FALLEN BROTHER IN BLUE:

The Tragic Death of
Boise Police Officer Mark Stall

FALLEN BROTHER IN BLUE:

The Tragic Death of
Boise Police Officer Mark Stall

By

Arnold Rubey

ACW Press
5501 N. 7th Ave. #502
Phoenix, AZ 85013

Publisher's Cataloging-in-Publication
(Provided by Quality Books, Inc.)

Rubey, Arnold.
    Fallen brother in blue: the tragic death of
    Boise police officer Mark Stall / [by Arnold Rubey
    — 1st ed.
      p. cm.
      ISBN 1-892525-15-1

      1. Stall, Mark Arlin—Death and burial.
    2. Police murders—Idaho—Boise.   3. Christian
    biography—Idaho—Boise. 4. Boise (Idaho). Police
    Department.   I. Title

HV8148.B652R83 2000   363.2'0979628
                      QBI99-1077

Printed in the United States of America

In dedication to

Cheryl Stall-Chamberlain

A courageous and loving wife
who through life and unexpected death
has nobly stood strong in faith and virtue;

and to

Jonelle and Julia Stall,

two wonderful and special girls who were the
apples of their father's eyes.
He loved you each with a devout love,
and now with courage and peace of heart
you can cherish the legacy left you
all your remaining days on earth

Contents

Special Thanks

A police death instantly draws a myriad of people into its centrifugal force. In the aftermath of Mark Stall's death, countless individuals and groups became part of the subsequent events. Their personal involvement forms the legacy of this story. The list is so extensive that it exceeds the ability of these writings to include anywhere near all that deserve to be acknowledged. However, these are specially singled out:

The Boise Police Department and Chief Larry Paulson who gave and gave to make sure Mark's funeral was a proper tribute for his sacrifice, and further insured that his widow and two daughters would be provided with memories and police involvement to whatever degree necessary for as long as necessary;

All Law Enforcement agencies throughout the nation, particularly the western United States who cared, came, and contributed extraordinary respect for a fellow officer;

The greater Boise community for their phenomenal public support and encouragement throughout the days and weeks following Mark's death;

Boise State University and its sacrificial Pavilion staff who on short notice provided and prepared their facilities so that all who desired could attend the funeral and witness a notable chapter in Boise's history;

The Boise Police Department Auxiliary which arranged meals and countless service to the family, including the hand-making of thousands of blue ribbons commemorating support for the police, and particularly for Mark's sacrifice;

Lake Hazel Baptist Church (recently renamed Lake Hazel Bible Church) for their sacrificial love and giving to the Stall family who were a cherished part of their fellowship, and whose entire church facility Mark voluntarily repainted a year before his death;

C.O.P.S. (Concerns Of Police Survivors) which provided national recognition for all 1997 fallen officers in Washington D.C. in May 1998, and also provided survivor seminars and specialized sessions for survivor families;

Ray and Nancy Stall—Mark's parents—for their strength, honor, and transparency in supporting their son's memory, and for their willingness to selflessly support Cheryl's future without their beloved son;

Matt Stall, Linda Olsen, and Louise Malone—Mark's brother and sisters—who freely opened their hearts to the Boise community to convey the qualities of their youngest brother whom they loved and respected;

Kay Rubey—Mark's mother-in-law and my wife—who often gave beyond her strength to be there for her daughter and grand-daughters, and who through her own pain, patiently endured a difficult year of reliving this tragedy so that this story could be written;

Almighty God—who in sovereign grace prepared Mark for eternity, then provided for his loved ones the strength needed to keep trusting in spite of their sorrow. They as a family abide in the assurance that Mark is safely home and that God has not erred in what He allowed. Therefore, to God be the glory both now and forever (2 Peter 3:18).

Foreword

This is a true story. It is about police work. It is about an officer's family. It is about his tragic death; and yet, it is about hope.

I have been a cop all of my adult life. I served 38 years with the Los Angeles Police Department. I have been there when officers have been shot… and killed. I have notified the family members. I have attended the funerals. I have witnessed the trauma to everyone involved in these sad events. I know from first hand experience how these crises play out. I have experienced the emotion, the shock and the grief. That is why I can tell you that this book is real.

Mark and Cheryl Stall began their life together excited about the future. Mark is doing what he always dreamed of doing. He is a police officer in a city where he can practice his chosen profession and still pursue a good quality of life. Boise, Idaho is in many ways a fulfillment of their dreams. The future is bright.

The author takes you into the family life of this young police couple. He does it with first hand knowledge and realism. Arnold Rubey is the father of Cheryl.

Then one horrible night Cheryl experiences what every police wife fears. Mark goes to work and never returns. He is involved in a fierce gun-battle that takes his life.

The gun-battle is described with amazing accuracy. Rubey combines the official tape recording of the violent encouter with the eye witness descriptions of the surviving officers and witnesses. You feel as though you are there. You experience the immediate reaction of the officers at the scene. You are in on the grim notification of Cheryl and the rest of the family. You attend the funeral and begin to understand that when an officer dies that way, it is only the beginning of grief and a lengthy process. Two young girls will grow up not really grief and a lengthy process. Two young girls will grow up not really knowing their father.

But this story has hope. In the midst of this sorrowful series of events, many wonderful and uplifting things happened. I saw some of them occur as I responded to a request to help the men and women of the Boise Police Department cope shortly after the tragedy. I saw many brother and sister officers moved to confront their own uncertainty about the future and their relationship with their Creator. Rubey thoughtfully brings in the dynamic of the spiritual dimension of this family. He illustrates the inner strength and comfort that only God can bring to people caught up in such a trying experience.

There are only two types of people in the world. Those who *have gone* through the deep waters of life, and those who *will go* through the deep waters of life's trials. This book will be an encouragement to both groups.

Bob Vernon
Assistant Chief of Police (ret.)
Los Angeles Police Department

Introduction

Almost every other day in America, a policeman dies in the line of duty. In 1997, one hundred sixty law enforcement officers gave their lives while carrying out their commissions on behalf of their states, counties, or cities. They all carried a badge and legally represented law enforcement in the jurisdictions where they served.

In no place is the high cost of this kind of sacrifice more broadly felt than in Judiciary Square in Washington, D.C., which contains the National Law Enforcement Officers Memorial. When the calendar year of 1997 ended, the two walls encompassing the Square would require the addition of those one hundred sixty names to those already there, for a new total of 14,662. All are individuals who have died in the line of duty since records have been kept, and the vast majority are from this century. Behind every etched name lies a story, a legacy, and a biography.

One of the new names on the wall is Mark Arlin Stall, who was shot to death in Boise, Idaho on September 20, 1997 in an extremely violent gun battle in the parking lot of a downtown Boise bar. He was the first police officer to lose his life in the line of duty in the over one-hundred-year history of the Boise Police Department.

Only four years earlier he had left the Los Angeles Sheriff's Department to continue his law enforcement career in a quieter, safer locality. That he would then lose his life in the city to which he felt thus drawn was an unthinkable prospect—after all, he had moved his family in order to live in a place more suited to raising them in security. That hope died when he died.

With so many deaths occurring in law enforcement—an average of one hundred fifty-five per year in the 1990's—why tell his particular story? Was his life so different or distinct from the thousands of

13

others whose names appear on the walls of Judiciary Square? In all likelihood, each life's story would have merited being more permanently recorded. However, few fallen officer biographies are written and preserved so that others may learn more. It is very important then that Mark Stall's story not be lost in this kind of obscurity. It is therefore told here, for several reasons.

One, the shock and circumstances associated with his killing became significant to the Boise community he served and in which he was living when he died. He was thereafter acknowledged for bravery, venerated for his sacrifice, and posthumously awarded many honors.

Two, the Boise community and the surrounding Treasure Valley region have maintained ongoing interest in Mark's personal and family life, and have also continued to be curious about details associated with the battlefield he and his fellow officers fought on that morning. Further interest was generated when his funeral was telecast to an estimated two million northwest homes.

Three, few fallen officers have their stories perpetuated in permanent form, aside from what appeared in print or film around the times of their deaths. As a result, the impact felt at the time of death slowly fades, and the costly sacrifices of these brave men and women tend to be forgotten as the years pass. In Mark's case, this book will preserve the account of his sacrifice for generations to follow. This is his written legacy.

Four, Mark Stall exuded integrity and character in both his personal and professional lives, which instantly endeared him to his community. Overnight he went from an obscure, taken-for-granted cop doing his usual job, to a celebrated hero who made the ultimate sacrifice. He was then memorialized for what he had been both in and out of uniform.

Finally, Mark's life, apart from the circumstances of his death, was in many ways a typical story of many law enforcement families in this country. They know about the typical cop's life—the mind set, the struggles and strains, and the sacrifices. Police life is unique, filled with challenges and experiences that those outside the calling seldom see or even know. Also, surprisingly few know or understand, even within law enforcement, what a police death and its aftermath does to a family, a community, or to themselves. Unless they have gone through it, or been close to it personally, even they cannot fathom the impact. But in every other way, these families identify with the life and struggles the Stall family faced on a daily basis.

In the few days between Mark's death and funeral, a portrait of him and his family was repeatedly printed in newspapers and telecast to the public. The photo depicted four handsome, smiling faces. Those faces stirred people's imaginations about what it must be like for two young daughters to be without their daddy, and a young widow to be without her husband. Those visual images emotionally bonded the hearts of thousands of strangers to the family of the slain officer.

This book, then, tells the story of that family and how they coped with this horrible and senseless loss. It further tells of others connected to this tragedy in their unique roles. It is not an easy read. The day-by-day experiences exposed herein are candid; the story and its conclusions, straightforward.

As you walk step by step through the ordeals faced by the family and the police, you will likely cry with them. In addition, you may feel anger at some of the unsavory facts detailed in these writings. But you will also be provided with hope and comfort, and will discover that even in a tragedy of this magnitude, the strength can be found to continue life's journey.

This book has been prayerfully and painstakingly written. Mark Stall's immediate and extended family, his many friends, his brothers in blue, and his Boise community are the foundation of the story; however, people in all vocations, in every place in this country, can and will relate to the human interest aspect of Mark Stall's story. It is the story of people who struggle to find meaning and hope in the aftermath of their loved one's death.

Finally, the most important chapter in this book is Chapter Seventeen. Those pages reflect the deeper meaning and message that Mark Stall's life and death provide for people in all walks of life. The rest of the story, however, will make that chapter all the more meaningful if read first. To that end, we begin a remarkable story.

1

September 19–The Day Before

$\mathbf{F}$riday morning in Boise, Idaho. Treasure Valley residents rose this warm September morning with the welcome awareness that this was for many of them the last workday of another week—their Thank-Goodness-It's-Friday. At the end of this day it would be let-down time—that much-anticipated time for another weekend of pleasant activities to which they could look forward. The Women's Fitness Celebration anticipated a big Saturday with thousands of women participating, and the Boise State University Broncos hoped to secure their first football victory under new head coach Houston Nutt.

In the Stall household, this was but the midway point of the workweek. Four ten-hour nights, beginning each Wednesday night, filled Mark Stall's typical work schedule, patrolling the streets of Boise in behalf of its 165,000 citizens. Two more nights remained on this week's schedule of nocturnal police work. When those two shifts were over and looked back on, they would in all probability be remembered as nondescript—there would be "little to write home about."

On the other hand, there had been recent situations in Boise, some tragic, that had placed this police department in the hot seat of scrutiny. From June 1996 to this date in September, a period of fifteen months, five shooting deaths in five separate incidents at the hands of the Boise police department had occurred. With this many violent, fatal encounters, attention on a national scale had been drawn to Boise's men in blue.

Even New York City Police Commissioner Howard Safir wrote in *Parade* magazine about it. Referring to his own city's efforts to crack down on crime, he boldly stated, "Right now, we're safer than Boise, Idaho."

The questions began, and seemed to continue nonstop. How could a moderate-sized city like Boise have so much violence in such a short time? Was this police department out of control and trigger-happy? What were the police doing to justify such drastic actions?

Each shooting occurred at night. Three of the incidents were before midnight, while the other two were early morning. Each took place during hours that Mark and his fellow night-team officers were on duty, or on nights they happened to be off and other team members were involved. No matter—the tensions in the aftermath of these incidents left a foul taste in both police and public minds. Bad things were happening in Boise. Since the police were first the responders, then the shooters who took a life, they automatically became the focus of attention and were questioned about their actions. In the minds of some outspoken people, the police had to be at fault—they were too aggressive. Little was said about those who drew the police into these situations, or about responsibility for the behavior that resulted in such terrible consequences.

Most had but faint memories of the stunning incident in Idaho in January 1994 when an officer from a neighboring city was sense-lessly shot to death a by a fourteen-year-old boy. The boy stole a car in Boise and drove it forty-five miles west to the community of New Plymouth. Wade Feldner, a New Plymouth policeman, spotted the car in his town sometime after midnight and pulled the driver over in a school parking lot. In a matter of seconds, Feldner's life was taken by this teenager, who callously shot him with a gun provided by a family member.

Mark well knew what he and his fellow officers were facing on the streets, and he resented how some elements of the public reacted to his police department. While he had not been directly involved in any of the previous incidents, he took the negative press personally. He was numbered among the men in blue—they were teammates—and as such he felt included in the critical comments. He and his friends were being made the scapegoats because of the manner in which they were forced to deal with the rebellion which they had been hired to confront. The lack of sympathy regarding the nature of the risks they encountered in their work wore heavily on their emotions.

As Officer Mark Stall, Ada #512 (his Ada County hire number), walked out of 7200 Barrister Drive on this beautiful Friday morning after his night shift, he could return to being Citizen Stall for a few hours. Thirteen hours later, he would again dress in blue, strap on all the necessary paraphernalia to carry out his work, then climb into a patrol car for the night's work. That was the routine.

This morning he was more than ready to get home and crash. He was very tired. Weariness was always a factor after working all night, but he had been pushing his limits by working paint jobs all spring and summer to put a dent in some debt. His days off, Monday through Wednesday, were often given to the side jobs.

His work was superb and, as a result, word of mouth brought him more work than he wanted or could even handle. However, he found it hard to say no, because some of these jobs were for family or friends. Those who didn't personally know him wanted him because he came highly recommended.

As fall approached, Cheryl, his wife of eight years, had become increasingly uptight at his being gone most of the time over the summer months. The girls also missed having their daddy around as much as they would like. As for Mark himself, he was more than tired of it—he wanted out of the painting business so he could come back to his family.

He tossed his duffel bag into the trunk and wearily plopped himself into the comfortable velour seat. Though his Olds Regency was nine years old and nearing 100,000 miles, it still gave a comfortable ride. It was a pleasure to drive, after long hours in a police car which had to accommodate umpteen different drivers and multi-sized bodies. As always, he made slight adjustments to his mirror and seat, then headed home.

Cheryl was still in bed since the girls were not yet awake. She was accustomed to sleeping alone four nights a week, and because of this often stayed in bed until Mark got home. If he was not delayed by late police activity, and the girls were still sleeping, it provided the two of them a small amount of time together before the new day got underway. Sometimes he stayed up long enough to see the girls, then slipped in earplugs to shut out the noises of the day. He was by then very ready to rest his tired body.

This Friday morning was a usual morning. Upon reaching home, he puttered in the kitchen a few moments, grabbed a bite to eat, then came in to bed. He and Cheryl had some time together, then she got up to let him get to sleep. When the girls later awakened, he was already out. They would have to wait until late afternoon to see him.

About 2:00, he awakened and briefly got up. When he headed back to bed, Julia, the three-and-a-half-year-old, spotted him. In her boisterous voice she shouted, "Daddy! Daddy!" She was excited to see him up. As she reached for a hug, she told him she loved him. Both the hugs and the "I love you, daddy," were common and meaningful expressions for both of Mark's girls. They adored their daddy and cherished every moment they could get with him. Of course, his "I love you, too," was special for them to get in return.

Mark adored his girls. Jonelle was born in Lancaster, California in 1991, when he worked in the Los Angeles Sheriff's Office. She was a big baby—nine-and-a-half pounds. Cheryl decided, after some fifteen hours of hard labor, that instead of the six kids they sometimes had talked about having, they would stop at one!

Jo was her mom all over again, and as would be expected, instantly became a sparkling joy to them. Of course, it didn't take long to reconsider the number of children they would like to have!

Julia was born in Boise in 1994, five months after Mark began with the Ada County Sheriff's Department. She was a pound smaller at birth than her sister. She had her dad's thinner frame and was his "spitting image." Her great-grandmother, after seeing her for the first time, stated that the only thing this girl needed to look exactly like her dad was a mustache!

At 4:30 p.m. Mark got up to stay. He found Cheryl downstairs working on household business matters. He plopped himself down, groaning about the difficulty of waking up.

"I had that dream again," he blurted out.

"And?" Cheryl asked.

"It was the same as usual. It always ends up the same way."

Cheryl said no more, because it was unpleasant for both of them to dwell on or even think about. Though he felt compelled to tell her about the dream when he first had it, she knew he didn't like talking about it because it threw unwarranted fear into her. After all, this was a mere dream and should not be considered something to be concerned about. Yet it continued to bother him, and Cheryl knew it did because he would periodically bring it up again.

It would just be a short time, however, before the frightening scenario he envisioned in his dream would stir an eerie, shuddering chill in Cheryl. Later, when she reluctantly shared the nature of Mark's dream with others, they, too, were stunned by the uncanny reality that had actually come to pass from his repetitious nightmare.

Cheryl headed to the kitchen to prepare dinner while Mark showered and prepared for the third night of his workweek. After that he played a game with the girls, which they always enjoyed because one or the other of them generally ended up the winner.

Mark gave the girls quality time when he could, but it just wasn't enough for them or him. His work on the streets of Boise for the city, and his painting and deck jobs consumed most of his available hours. With fall coming, however, he had decided to wind down on the extra jobs. He intended to enjoy the winter months with his family. They were ready, and so was he.

After dinner, both girls said, "May I please be excused?" and "Thank you, Mommy, for the delicious dinner." Both Mark and Cheryl had been teaching them simple manners, and to express appreciation to those who did nice things for them. In this case they thanked their mother for feeding them. Since she and Mark had just completed a parenting class for the second time, they were encouraged to see their daughters respond to the nurturing they were placing into in their young lives.

Following dinner, Mark helped Cheryl clear the table and clean up the kitchen. Soon everything was in its place again.

Ever the perfectionist, Mark was driven to be clean and orderly. It was a trait that distinguished him on the police force as well. He was known to wipe down the interior of the car he was about to drive on patrol, and to do it again at the end of his shift. His propensity for neatness never changed, though he learned over time to be less driven to make everything right at the immediate moment he saw the need!

Cheryl had adjustments to make in their relationship, since she was in no way driven to be a neat-nick like Mark. She tended to be less orderly and more relaxed. This difference in their dispositions created some tensions between them; however, they helped each other by providing some balance to each other's tendencies.

A few moments yet remained before Mark had to leave for work. He decided they would rekindle the festive spirit they had enjoyed nine days before when celebrating Jo's sixth birthday. In short order they were running around the living room playing Freeze, and as always with these two active girls, giggles and laughter filled the house.

Cheryl watched the fun. During Freeze, they danced to oldies tunes like Elvis Presley's "Jailhouse Rock" and "Won't You Be My Teddy Bear?" As she admiringly watched what she called her "goofy family," she had to admit these girls had an awesome daddy. She had recently been uptight about how little time they had together, and even this night she was sulking about it. Yet she appreciated her hard-working husband and loving dad giving meaningful moments to his girls. Little did they know then how special these last few moments together on this particular Friday night would become to the three ladies of the house.

As the dancing continued, the doorbell rang. It was the Schwan's man. Mark usually did not place large orders for Schwan's excellent ice cream, but he was certainly one of the most faithful in placing some kind of order. He was ready this night with a larger order than usual, because he and Cheryl had plans. They would need enough ice cream on Tuesday evening the twenty-third to serve several couples, who were coming to their house after the Clay Crosse Concert at the Boise State University Pavilion. They all had tickets and were excited about the concert and looking forward to spending the evening together.

Mark wrote a check to Schwan's for $26.75—the last written document from his hand. It was vintage Mark on his checks—after neatly printing all the pertinent information, he then signed with his almost illegible signature. At the top of the check he printed the date: 9-19-97.

Finally he had to go. It was 8:15 p.m. He liked being at the station in ample time to not be hurried in getting ready for his shift. While he was prompt when it came to work, he was much more relaxed outside work. He often misjudged time when it came to keeping a schedule, and many times kept people waiting and wondering where he was. It was as though he needed some detachment from pressure, including time pressures, outside his police work, so he hung loose when it came to punctuality. While it was more relaxing for him, it was frustrating for others. It was, however, one of the few weaknesses in the life of a talented, respected, zestful young man.

Everyone got the usual hug and kiss. Mark then dashed out the door to the garage.

"Gotta go. See you in the morning." He jumped into the car, quickly backed out, then honked at the girls when he reached the street. As usual, they were standing in the window waving and blowing kisses to him.

He would not come home to see them the next morning, or give them one more hug, or tell them ever again that he loved them. He would not again see daylight.

2

September 19—The Last Night

It was almost dark as Cheryl and the girls watched the car quickly disappear from sight. Mark usually took their family sedan to the station, or had Cheryl drop him off, since their other vehicle, a 1970 Chevy pickup, needed brake work. He wasn't about to pay someone to do the job when he could do it himself, but he had been too busy to get to it. He used the pickup for his paint jobs, but beyond that it was driven very little. Since he would be back home before the car would be needed Saturday morning, he drove himself to the station.

Jo and Julia got ready for bed, after which Cheryl read them some stories. They then prayed together, as they customarily did each night at bedtime. When Mark was home at bedtime, it was usually he who tucked them in and prayed with them. This night, as always in their prayers, they asked that their daddy and husband would have a good night at work, and that he and his fellow officers would be kept safe.

Finally the house grew quiet. The stillness was welcome to Cheryl after the noisy evening of games and giggles. She was ready for some time to herself, so she propped up pillows and climbed into bed, ready to do some reading. Before she could get into the mood to read, however, she had to work through some ill feelings she had about Mark being gone from them so much these past few months. She and the girls really needed and wanted him to them-selves for a change, and she was sulking about his caring for every-one else's desires instead. As she lay there, she kept mulling these things over in her mind and emotions.

She knew he worked hard—he always did, but that did not relieve her frustrations. In spite of her grumpiness, she could not honestly fault his generous spirit to others, nor his conscientious work ethic. Mark always found it hard to say no if he felt something could and should be done; and when he said yes, he made sure he finished the job and finished it right.

Mark was California born and raised. His parents, Ray and Nancy Stall, raised four children, with Mark the youngest. Upon graduation from Monta Vista High School in Cupertino in 1986, he enrolled at the Master's College, 300 miles downstate in Newhall. It was there that he would cross paths with a girl from Colorado, Cheryl Rubey, though when they met he was seriously involved with someone else. It would be two more years before they would come to see each other in a different light, with future thoughts beyond friendship.

In December 1988, during her junior year at the Master's College, Cheryl found herself needing work on a 1977 Camaro she had recently purchased. The Camaro replaced the 1963 VW bug she had wrecked a few weeks earlier in a near-tragic incident in Canyon Country. She had learned that Mark, whom she knew casually at that time, was mechanically inclined. In spite of not knowing him well, she was bold enough to ask him to look at it for her. Since she was living off-campus with her parents, who were located only a few miles from the college, she made arrangements for Mark to come to their house to check over the car. She let him in, then had to leave for a while, trusting the place to him. When Cheryl's mother, Kay, later returned from being gone herself, she found this unknown man in the garage with the engine of Cheryl's car on the floor. He hastened to tell her who he was and that Cheryl had invited him there to work on the car. He found that he had to rebuild the engine and in several days had it up and running. Cheryl, when she could, worked alongside him during those days.

This became Cheryl's first experience with the skills of Mark Stall. As the years passed, others came to admire the innate abilities of this young man—if something needed fixing, Mark could do it. If he didn't know how, he asked or researched until he found the answer, then proceeded to accomplish the task. He had an inquisitive mind and was fascinated by the challenge of fixing things. He learned well from his father, who by his own diligence taught his children honesty and hard work.

The car situation established the beginning of a mutual attraction, and they found themselves increasingly drawn to one another. The car brought them together, but God drew them together. Thereafter, falling in love came surely and swiftly.

Shortly after the car repair, Cheryl informed her mother that she knew whom she was going to marry, and that she would in fact be married within a year. His name? Mark Stall.

Mark went to his parent's home in Cupertino that Christmas, and wrote back to Cheryl about what was going on in his heart. He admitted he had fallen for her, but didn't quite understand how and why this was happening to him. He wrote:

> "Even though it's so early in the `game' for `us', I have had a strong feeling for wanting this to work stronger than I've ever felt. I don't understand it—I don't really know you, but the desire is there.
>
> God knows my heart and is expecting my best from me in my plans and my decisions as to the choice of life that I'll make.
>
> I've told myself and God that I was committed to Him to make the full decision about my love/spouse and that He was the true author of my life and the founder of my future."

In February 1989, Cheryl asked Mark if he would "marry her" for the Marriage and Family class she was taking at the college. They would role-play a wedding in front of the class. He agreed.

Two months later, on April 4, Cheryl's assignment for the same class was to discuss "all the baggage I would bring into a marriage." Since this was a night class, she asked Mark if he would come and listen to her presentation. He said he would try, but it might be hard to pull off since he had just started police academy for the Los Angeles Sheriff's Department.

He showed up on campus before class, but informed her he couldn't stay because the Academy had bogged him down with homework for the next day. Disappointed, she watched him head to the parking lot. Then she watched him stop and talk to some of the guys who were in her class. When they finally showed up, the class was well underway, and she figured she could have had her presentation already given if it would have helped him get away quickly.

Now she was more than disappointed—she was ticked off. But she reminded herself that this was a trademark of the man she was falling in love with—he loved to talk!

Midway through class, the guy next to her suddenly got up and left. He was back shortly, holding a beautiful bouquet of roses, which he then presented to Susan Odekerken, the professor. Susan acted excited to get them, but then announced they were not for her, but for someone else in the class. Cheryl idly wished that someone special would get her roses someday.

The professor then began reading aloud a letter attached to the bouquet:

> *To the woman that God has blessed me with:*
> *Our friendship has grown ever so fast. The times we spend together are so precious to me. You've become my best friend by just being you, and I like the "you" I see! God has blessed me with you and all that you are: gentle, loving, thoughtful, fun, exciting, and most of all, you truly love our Lord. I can see what special care God has put into feeding you and raising you into a wonderful woman of God. I feel so blessed to be a part of your life, and to think that you might want to spend your life with me—just you, me, and God. Ever since we got married in this class last month, I've felt God telling me in so many ways that you are "the one" He has "reserved" for me. So what do you think?*
> *Inside this bouquet, tied to the stem of a rose, is a ring that I want you to wear forever and ever! Cheryl Kay Rubey, will you marry me? Forever your ????, Mark*

It took a moment for Cheryl to assimilate what had just happened. She had just been given a proposal by a beau who was not even present! She was then asked to come to the front of the class. As she shakily came to her feet, someone called from the back, "Is that a yes?"

"Yes!" she exclaimed. But where was her suitor?

She moved forward to look for the ring Mark had hidden in the bouquet. As she did, the man "bogged down with homework" poked his head in a side door and asked if her "yes" was his cue!

He joined her at the front, and together they found the ring, which he then placed on her finger. They hugged, too embarrassed to cause a scene by kissing. The class erupted in applause and cheers.

They were married six months later on September 2, 1989 at Grace Community Church in Sun Valley, California. Cheryl's dad, a pastor, gave her away and conducted part of the ceremony. Mark Stall and Cheryl Rubey became one that day and began their antici-pated long life together.

Their first year of marriage was rough. Mark had been sworn into the Los Angeles Sheriff's Office (LASO) a month before their wedding, and began work in minimum security at the Wayside Honor Rancho, a county jail, a few miles north of Newhall. They immediately began the challenge of simultaneously adapting to sev-eral new things—a new law enforcement career, a new place to live, and a new marriage.

They found themselves frequently disagreeing and arguing, but they rode out the tossing waves of that first year and began to grow stronger in their relationship. Although they found that adjusting to law enforcement work made them both testy, they had tried to men-tally prepare themselves beforehand for the challenges they might face. They were striving to keep themselves from crashing on the rocky path they had now begun to experience together.

They had talked extensively about the hardships in this kind of life during the months before their marriage. Mark was in the acad-emy during their engagement, which provided a small taste of what their future life might be like. They, just like others before them, could not know in the beginning what they would later learn first-hand about the stresses of Mark's chosen vocation. And they could never prepare for the ultimate test—loss of life on the job. But the likelihood of that was unthinkable, though they both knew it was possible.

One characteristic among police families is the high rate of divorce. The percentage of couples breaking up is high because of the unique pressures associated with the job. Continual exposure to unruly people can begin the build up of certain resentments towards society in general. In turn, the family, particularly a spouse, absorbs the brunt of that growing cynicism when her husband vents frus-tration over stressful happenings.

Compensation issues can further add to the burden of the job, and subsequently to a marriage. In some cities the police department copes with city or county leaders who tend to make their law enforcement personnel feel less than worthy of the respect they deserve. One particular way this happens is to play tight on budget considerations for the police. In light of the higher-risk roles law enforcement personnel are called upon to perform for the community, it is unfortunate this kind of attitude exists in the decision-making levels of government. Many police officers need to take on second jobs to supplement their income, which in the earlier years of their careers can be quite meager in respect to the required skills and potential dangers they face due to their line of work. Low pay and high risk are not very compatible, and the toll makes itself felt in the marriages.

These kinds of struggles and factors create an invisible, very negative impact on dedicated and hard-working officers and their families. When they fail to adequately deal with these and other problems, they become prime candidates for serious marital problems.

Work-related tensions among officers are often brought home and unloaded on a spouse, the kids, or the dog. On the other hand, there is also the danger of too little communication between spouses. An officer may choose to shield his wife (or husband, as the case may be) from some of the unsavory things with which he must deal, so he holds those things in and shuts her out. It takes a strong and understanding wife to hold up and not cave in.

Cheryl did not enter into marriage with Mark believing it would be an idyllic life, but she and he both believed they could handle life's challenges with God's help added to their own efforts. Mark truly believed his work as a policeman could be conducted through God's strength if both he and Cheryl chose to trust Him and each other. Through the early years of their young marriage, they continued to learn that they would need to work steadily at their relationship if it was to be all they hoped it might.

They first and foremost determined to beat the odds of losing their marriage by eliminating divorce as an option. Instead, they determined to establish a bond that would remain unbroken throughout their planned lifetime together.

The increased safety risk because of the nature of Mark's job was another factor with which they had to cope. Cheryl had no inkling of what it might be like should something happen to him. They had planned to stay together through love, and hoped they would not prematurely separate through death. The first was fulfilled; the second was not to be.

As Cheryl mused on these things this Friday night, she finally decided to stop being upset and get to her reading. She was drawn to two magazine articles that her mother-in-law, Nancy Stall, had sent her some weeks earlier. Nancy often found helpful things to read, and when she did, she copied them and shared them with family or friends.

The first was, "How God Answers Prayer." The author emphasized that God answers prayer in the ways He does so that He can draw rightful glory to Himself through the answer provided. This does not make God an egotist, as some might conclude, but rather it acknowledges His supremacy as God and emphasizes His worth. He is truly worthy of our respect, and because of this we can have faith in the nature of His answers in our behalf.

Cheryl, from her reading, began to reflect on how she prayed for Mark. For one thing, she regularly asked God to protect him on the job. She had also been praying another kind of prayer: she petitioned God to make her husband a good example and testimony to those whose lives he touched throughout the community, and for him to be a positive influence to his brothers in blue. The article before her affirmed in her mind that she should continue praying as she had in the past, while being content to leave the results to God. He would accomplish His purposes in His way, and could be trusted to do right in whatever He brought to pass. How little she knew how great a test awaited her regarding her trust in God.

She then moved to the second article, "How to Be A Submissive Wife." The title initially annoyed her. Not that she did not believe in proper submission to her husband, but since she had been grouchy with him, she was feeling anything but submissive. Throughout the day now ending, she had struggled with this. She had to continually remind herself that Mark was working his heart out to provide extra for them as a family, nonetheless she was resentful about the time-cost of that extra work—he was gone too much, particularly these past few months.

In spite of the title, she read on. Strangely, after moving only part way into the article, she found herself convinced that she really did need to show stronger honor to Mark, and by the time she finished the article, her heart had become soft and tender about this. She felt surprisingly different than she had a few moments earlier.

She glanced at the clock—it was past midnight. In spite of the hour, Mark was out there on the streets somewhere, and she felt very pressed to talk to him and to do so as soon as possible. She paged him, then waited.

Within minutes, he called. They talked for a moment, after which Cheryl opened up and shared what was in her heart. She told him she knew she had not been acting right toward him and wanted his forgiveness; that she had been grouchy and had failed to give him his proper honor. Further, she didn't want him to be bothered about things at home so that it would affect his work—his task was hard enough as it was. She told him she wanted to do better and to be more supportive of his efforts to adequately provide for them as a family.

Mark's response was positive. He told her he appreciated her saying these things, and for trying to understand his heart. He too wanted everything right between them.

In those few moments, early in the morning of September 20, their jaded relationship was renewed. They were reconciled with each other.

With things now right with her man, Cheryl could lie down and sleep in peace. All was well between them.

As they closed their conversation, they did so with their usual, "Love you," and Mark returned to the streets with his partner. It was the last time Cheryl would hear his voice.

3

September 20–Early Morning

Night hours in the city—any city—bring on more than streetlights and draw out more than normal nighttime functions. Nocturnal activities begin churning among certain individuals with not-so-honorable mind-sets, people who find the dark period of the 24-hour cycle their optimum time for action, as they engage in not-so-upright activities or wander around the city with time to kill. Darkness is their welcome ally, and they utilize the cover of night to conceal what they do.

Unsavory night behavior is not a problem unique to the twentieth century. It existed centuries before Christ. Solomon alluded to this in Proverbs 4:14-17: *"Do not enter the path of the wicked, and do not walk in the way of evil. Avoid it, do not travel on it; turn away from it and pass on. For they do not sleep unless they have done evil, and their sleep is taken away unless they make someone fall. For they eat the bread of wickedness, and drink the wine of violence."* People have long used the night to be less noticeable and to cover evil deeds.

As night deepens, this element of the population may imbibe alcoholic beverages, perhaps do some drugs, or, if nothing else, get their emotions stirred up over subjects about which they are wound tight. They build up steam regarding what they don't like in society, and frequently what they don't like is authority figures. The struggle with authorities has become more pronounced in the latter part of this century, especially in more heavily populated areas. Dislike of governing officials is an issue everywhere, even in secluded mountain areas; but cities with dark, sheltered drinking establishments, in a strange but provocative way, supply a gathering place for kindred spirits to share their discontent with others who think and feel as they do. It is often in these environments that anti-authority attitudes and talk stir things up, and already edgy dispositions are further agitated. This is especially true for young men.

When it comes to authorities, cops sit on the top of the list of those especially despised by less-savory citizens. Their presence on the streets and by-ways of the community is conspicuous, and as a result, they represent an unwelcome obstacle to shady activities. Because of what the police symbolize—law and order—they are viewed with disdain, for they hinder or interfere with illegal activities and evil plans. The police are therefore made the enemy—the foes that you resist or fight if necessary.

Nighttime officers know that this is how the streets and activities of the city function after dark. Not every night is equally as busy or intense, but the other side of day becomes the choice time for certain elements within the community to engage in unlawful or rowdy behavior.

A review of the five incidents that had occurred since June 1996 which involved the taking of lives by the Boise police department graphically reveals the truth of this perspective. Each and every encounter occurred at night—two of them before midnight, and three in the early morning hours after midnight.

Mark was a nighttime officer. He preferred nights, as do many officers; they welcome the challenge of dealing with the community during those hours. The larger part of his nine years in law enforcement was on graveyard hours. As a result, he became well acquainted with the idiosyncrasies of cities at night, including the city of Boise.

Prior to his move to Boise, after three years in the jails, he went on patrol in West Hollywood, California for two years. This unique geographical area of only two square miles is patrolled by the Los Angeles Sheriff's Office, although the city department, the Los Angeles Police Department (LAPD), patrols everything surrounding it. West Hollywood is composed of remarkably diverse populations. It includes a Russian community complete with its own Russian

Mafia activities, numerous gay bars, transvestites freely milling the streets nightly, and Sunset Boulevard, which is lined with teen hangouts to accommodate the hundreds of young people who frequent their establishments on weekends.

Mark's coming of age in law enforcement took place in West Hollywood. He learned an immense amount while working the jails, but the streets of West Hollywood provided him with an additional dimension of weird and memorable situations. Sometimes he freely talked about his experiences there; at other times he said little. Other than the time he spent with a training officer, he worked the long night shift in that unusual city.

One family member, after an all-night ride-along in West Hollywood with Mark, commented that his demeanor changed the instant he walked into the station for the night's work.

"He tensed up. His more relaxed self abruptly tightened up when he went through the door. He became very serious at that moment, and began to mentally adjust to what might face him that night."

There was another facet to his West Hollywood experience. He and Cheryl lived seventy miles from work. They had purchased a home in Lancaster while he was still in the jails because it provided the closest affordable housing area for couples getting started. Since he had been assigned to West Hollywood, however, he faced a grueling commute. Each shift was twelve hours, followed by the long ride home in the morning. He practically needed toothpicks to keep his eyelids open.

When a patrol position opened up in Lancaster, which was part of LA County, he requested consideration for the position. However, the sheriff's department did not accommodate his desire to work closer to home. In a confusing decision, they elected to keep him in West Hollywood and to assign another officer from the West Hollywood area to Lancaster!

Eventually he reached a point of wanting out of West Hollywood. Although he appreciated his colleagues, various aspects of the work there became a personal downer. Cheryl, too, was aware of the nature of some of his work there, and had difficulty being comfortable with it. They both came to a point at which they agreed it was time for a change.

Word got around that there were openings for new hires in Boise, Idaho. When Mark heard this, he called Boise to verify this information. Upon receiving confirmation that they were hiring, he scraped together the needed money to fly there and apply. He quickly found, however, that interest in coming to Boise also existed in numerous other places in the country. Competition to gain a spot in the city department was stiff, but he was determined, and decided he would keep trying even if he was not hired right away.

After his initial visit, his heart was even more set on Boise. For one thing, his mother-in-law was raised on a dairy farm an hour west of Boise, and her parents still lived in that same area. For another, Cheryl had often visited her grandparents in Idaho, and both knew and liked the area. Still another factor involved the likelihood of Cheryl's parents relocating to Idaho during this same time. If he and Cheryl followed them to Idaho, they would have for themselves and their children not only parents and grandparents, but even great-grandparents, as nearby parts of their lives. Family closeness was an attractive consideration.

Another factor that weighed heavily in Mark's thinking had to do with LA itself. He had experienced, as a deputy, the stark terror of the 1992 riots in Los Angeles in the aftermath of the Rodney King situation. The ugly and frightening series of violent incidents throughout the city hastened his resolve to leave. Both he and Cheryl agreed that they wanted a friendlier, safer environment in which to raise their family. Wherever they would go, even if Boise did not end up being that place, they still wanted to relocate where they would feel content to spend the rest of their lives. Boise, however, looked best for what seemed to them to be all the right reasons.

Being hired by the Boise Police Department did not materialize in his hoped-for time frame, nor were there assurances it would happen at all. He did reasonably well on his tests, but so did others. The next time he came to Boise to again test for a city position, he found that the Ada County Sheriff's department was also in the process of hiring. Since the Sheriff's department worked out of the same building as the city department, it would at least get them to Boise. From there, they could determine what their next options might be.

He decided to apply, knowing he would again be assigned to the jails for a while if hired. He had more than tired of dealing with the jail population while in LA, but it was a requirement for new hires in Ada County. He was offered a deputy's position, to begin in November 1993, which he accepted. He remained hopeful, however, that he might make the city department in the future if God willed and circumstances made it possible. He wanted to be on patrol.

When they headed to Boise, Cheryl was pregnant with their second child. Julia Rae was born five-and-a-half months after their arrival. They moved into a new triplex apartment, which served as their first Boise residence for eight months. At that point, they and Cheryl's parents pooled their money to purchase a large enough home for both families. They lived together in that home for two and a half years, after which Cheryl's parents bought another home not far away. Mark and Cheryl kept the original house, as it was spacious enough for a growing family.

A year after his arrival, Mark was offered a patrol position with the city of Boise, which he unhesitatingly accepted. He had finally attained what he had long been hoping would "be in the cards." He was now a brother in blue.

On December 8, 1994, he was sworn in by Chief Larry Paulson before a handful of family members and friends. Officers Ron Allex and Mark Vucinich were also sworn in that day. It was a happy time for the Stalls. As pictures were taken and congratulations extended, Officer Mark Stall began the process of adjusting to and settling in to the position that he had so looked forward to filling.

He worked graveyard for most of the next three years. During those many nights patrolling Boise with his fellow officers, he and they watched a quieter, mid-sized city expand in population and business growth. Also escalating in the community was the level of crime activity. During the summer of 1997, he verbalized his concerns about this trend to several people. Boise, he said, was beginning to face somewhat different things than it had in the past. While it had been just under four years since he had come to the city, he was troubled by the extreme deterioration that he observed taking place there. Unsavory outside influences were making their way into the fiber of the community.

One July day that summer, he engaged his father-in-law, Arnold Rubey, in a serious discussion about what he perceived to be happening on the streets of Boise. He seemed preoccupied about the situation, and it was obvious that what was taking shape in the city was of no little consequence to him.

"Boise is changing," he said, " in a not-so-good way. The kind of stuff over which I left LA is beginning to show up here. The people in the community do not see this, nor do they understand how serious it is becoming, but those of us on the streets know. Gangs and drug-related undesirables are moving in here, as well as increasing numbers of other problem-people. The stakes are getting raised higher every month."

Little could it be known that already present in the city was a young man from a distant state who would be joined by his brother ten weeks later to tragically validate Mark's concerns about wrongly-motivated people. Craig Brodrick of Pennsylvania had moved to Boise two months earlier in May, and his younger brother, Doug, would arrive in August. Mark Stall, a Boise policeman who sensed these kinds of possibilities and talked about people like them that July day, would fall victim to their callous and careless violence in the parking lot of a local night spot. They would soon destroy his life and bring devastation to his family.

After Friday night's briefing, the night team took to their cars and to their areas of responsibility. Mark and his partner, Rob Berrier, had car #81 this night. When possible, the department prefers two-man teams for the busier weekend nights. Teams provide an extra measure of safety for the officers and also present a stronger police presence should unusual situations arise.

On this shift, Mark and Rob were on directed patrol, as were other units that night. This meant they were to patrol a particular area. They would, of course, be on call wherever needed, but on this Friday night they were to cover downtown as part of a police contingent in the vicinity of young cruisers who typically fill downtown streets on weekend nights. Normally, Mark and Rob would work the bench, which was away from downtown. They had just moved from the valley to the bench two weeks earlier when reassignments had been made.

Since they were in the inner city, they stopped at the downtown substation at around 10:00 p.m. The substation, primarily used for curfew violations and as a holding area for juveniles, had a few light recreation games like Foosball and Ping-Pong. Occasionally officers stop in to gobble up homemade goodies provided by whoever is on duty that night, and to have a short "light-time" before going back on the streets.

Mark, Rob, and a couple of other officers engaged in a quick, rowdy game of Foosball, with Mark and his partner on the losing end. "Oh, rats!" he said, a familiar response when ending up on the wrong end of whatever he was doing. His two girls were also known to say, "Oh, rats!" during play times. Like father, like daughters.

Shortly, they were back on the streets.

Sometime after midnight, Mark's pager went off. It was Cheryl. They were just then driving into the Stinker station at Twenty-third and Main, one of their usual stops and also one of the places where the department fuels their vehicles.

Mark asked permission to use the inside phone, and dialed home. Cheryl tried to avoid unnecessary calls or pages while he was on duty, but occasionally found it comforting to talk with him during the long night hours. Tonight, however, was a night she had to talk to him. Little could he know how cherished this call would become to his soon-to-be widow. It would provide her a solace and comfort for the hard days ahead.

As Mark listened, Cheryl shared thoughts about things she needed to resolve with him. She had been crossways with him, and did not want the night to pass without making things right.

This conversation would soon become indelibly etched in her memory. It came about by God's precise timing and because of His divine providence. For her to call when she did, and for Mark to be at this station at that time, could only be orchestrated by God. They talked for a few minutes, then ended the call with each telling the other of their love.

It was back again to the streets. Soon a 911 call regarding a gun incident at the nearby Torch Lounge took them and several other units to that location. Two men had been escorted from the bar after one of them had been seen with a gun. After getting a rundown on the situation, those police units moved out into the city and passed on known information to other units about the incident. They would shortly encounter two men who fit the description of the two thrown out of the Torch.

About 1:00 a.m., Mark and Rob drove into the Chevron station at Sixteenth and State for ice cream. It was always hard for Mark to pass up ice cream, and this night was no exception. As they left the store, they told the clerk they'd probably be back later for a pastry, another hard-to-pass-up favorite.

Convenience stores appreciate the drive-bys and occasional drive-ins of police officers, especially at night. It gives them an enhanced safety factor and also allows them the opportunity to show appreciation to police personnel for their often-thankless work. Coffee, sodas, and other items are sometimes provided at reduced costs for the officers.

As car #81 again nosed onto the streets, it would be mere moments before a radio call from another downtown team would shape and change the community experience of Boise forever. As a city, they were about to embark on a new level of public adversity and community sorrow.

As for Mark Stall—he was about to lose his life at the hands of the kind of people he feared were in the city and up to no good.

4

The Battlefield

The Torch, advertised as Boise's only full liquor and food exotic dance club, is also called a "bikini bar." Those who frequent the Torch are there to hang out, spend time with friends, drink, or take in the skin show. As with any typical bar, it is rather dark. Alcohol and edgy dispositions sometimes trigger already loose tempers, foster fights, or stimulate havoc of some kind. Sometimes it is not alcohol that is the culprit, but rather it is the attitude, the chip on the shoulder, the desire to prove something.

Sometime past midnight on Friday night/Saturday morning, several dozen patrons were in the bar. A group of men who had been at another nightspot decided to stop at the Torch, also. When they entered, they found a table and sat down.

Immediately, two men approached them and told them they would have to move—this was their table. An argument ensued, after which one of the men from the larger group sought out the club bouncer for help. The bouncer told him that the other guys did in fact have that particular table, and had probably just been elsewhere for a while.

The issue settled in his mind, the man went back to the table and extended his hand to the more vocal of the two, to say no hard feelings. The man, scraggly-looking and sporting long, dark hair including facial hair, rose to his feet. He "got in the face" of the apologizer and proceeded to tell him that he was a cop and that he was this far—holding two fingers closely together—from arresting him. When asked for what, he replied "Drunk and disorderly." More flippant remarks were exchanged between them, after which they separated.

Somewhere in the course of these heated exchanges, the second of the two reclaiming their table made some ominous comments, which were overheard by at least one of the guys in the group. "Don't mess with my brother tonight," he said. "He's dangerous and he is going to go ballistic on somebody." He also stated that he held a third-degree black belt in Karate.

Not long afterwards, two men were reported to have been forcibly removed from the bar by the establishment. The size of the crowd and the low lights made it hard to be positive about identification, but several witnesses stated that the two tossed out were the brothers. One of them was seen to have a gun, which was the cause of their removal. As soon as they were out, the bouncers locked the doors and said, "Call the cops. Call the cops now." A call was then placed to police dispatch reporting the incident.

Within minutes, several uniforms descended on the Torch to get details. Among them were Officers Rob Berrier and Mark Stall, and Officers Bryan Hagler and Steve Van Doren, who were also a TAC team that night. Other officers came by the Torch as well during this time. After obtaining what information they could, general descriptions of the two ejected men were circulated among all the night officers, and they scattered to do patrol again. Downtown patrol units went on the look for the two men, either on foot or in a vehicle on the streets.

About 1:15 a.m., not long after the Torch incident, Hagler and Van Doren were driving west on Idaho Street, a one-way westbound street with three lanes. At Sixth and Idaho, they noticed an older-model car with an unusual or out-of-state license plate. Since they were too far back to read the plate, they pulled closer to the vehicle, which was occupying the center lane. They took the left lane and approached the rear of the car. It had a Pennsylvania plate.

They also noticed something else unusual. The car, a 1977 Chevy Impala, had been brush-painted over its entire surface with what appeared to be dull grey primer, plus its back bumper was painted black.

Hagler and Van Doren then moved into the center lane behind

the Impala. They tried running a plate check, but the radio channel was active, which delayed immediate access to information. They then started to punch in plate numbers on their portable computer, or Mobile Data Terminal, when the car they were following abruptly changed to the left lane without signaling. They moved behind the vehicle and continued to follow. Again, the driver made another rapid, unsignaled turn—this time into the parking lot of the Rider's Bar at Fifteenth and Idaho.

At this point Hagler who was driving the patrol car, switched on the overheads and pulled into the lot behind him. The driver veered his car somewhat toward the right after entering, since there were few cars in the lot. This kept their patrol car at somewhat of an angle to the suspect vehicle, yet safely behind. Van Doren immediately noted his angle to the passenger side of the suspect vehicle just in case.

Hagler then turned a spotlight on the vehicle. As he did, both front doors of the car flew open, and two male occupants emerged, one from each side. They began moving toward the police car only to have Hagler, who was now out of the car, order them back into their car. They continued to advance. Van Doren, who had opened his door and was placing his right leg on the ground, joined Hagler in ordering them back.

Both men seemed taken aback, as though they were not expecting a second officer. Hagler and Van Doren continued to shout commands to return to their car. Finally, they halted their movements toward the police car and complied with the commands given them. A nearby witness later reported that the men were told four or five times to get back into their car, and it was only after they were told they would go to jail if they did not comply that they reluctantly did what they were told.

The two officers still knew nothing about this car or its occupants, since everything had happened so quickly. However, they were now even more suspicious—the aggressive behavior of both men coming toward them, then their reluctance to comply with orders given them, caused Hagler and Van Doren to request two assist units. Also, at a glance these two were a possible fit for the description of the men escorted out of the Torch Lounge.

Police use three priority assist-codes to delineate the kind of help needed in the field. The lowest in urgency is Code One, which means assistance is needed but the situation is not critical. Code

Two calls for a response as quickly as possible but without lights or sirens. Code Three is the most crucial—it means there is a serious situation underway, assistance is needed immediately, and get there ASAP with lights and sirens.

Corporal Dale Rogers was at Eighth and Idaho, some seven blocks away, when Hagler's Code One assist call was issued. He immediately radioed that he was on his way. Rogers, a twenty-one-year veteran of the Boise police department, was in the K-9 unit, since he usually worked a dog on canine patrol. This night, however, he did not have his dog, but he did have his 22-year-old daughter, Cameo Adams, as a ride-along.

While they waited for assist units, Hagler and Van Doren kept a close watch on the occupants inside the car. Hagler moved over to a pickup parked somewhat parallel with the suspect's car. From there he could better observe their movements and provide himself cover if necessary. As he watched, he noticed both men moving their shoulders as if doing something in their laps. They also did a lot of talking and kept looking around.

Dale Rogers arrived, and pulled his car behind Hagler and Van Doren's cruiser. Hagler gave Rogers a rundown on why they had stopped this car and what he and Van Doren had been observing since the stop. They all agreed that they should conduct a high-risk stop, which meant getting both the driver and the passenger out of the car one at a time, then individually searching them. When they brought them out, they would move them away from the car and into the open, where officers could more safely approach them to search for any weapons that might be on them.

At this point, Officer Ron Winegar pulled up and parked on Idaho Street. He also had a ride-along this night, Stephanie Berry, a records clerk. Hagler now had his requested assist units, and four officers on scene. However, since other units were still in the general area due to the Torch Lounge incident, two other officer units rolled up as well.

Officer Gary Wiggins came next. He was alone. He also parked his car on Idaho Street, nosing toward Winegar's car. And finally, Mark Stall and Rob Berrier pulled up and parked parallel to Winegar on Idaho Street. They all had on their overheads for safety, since three patrol cars were occupying a couple of lanes in the street. There were now five patrol cars, seven officers, and two ride-alongs.

When Mark and Rob pulled up and saw all the cars there, Mark said to Berrier, "We won't be here long. They've got plenty of guys."

They exited their car and walked onto the sidewalk which ran along the front part of the parking lot. They asked what was going down. After being briefed on the situation and talking it over for a minute, Mark said, "We're outta here."

He and Rob turned back toward their patrol vehicle to leave, then they heard Bryan Hagler begin the process of getting the suspects out of their car. They halted their departure when Hagler shouted, "Driver."

They reasoned, "We're already here. We might just as well stay to see this through." They both turned back and moved toward the suspect car. As they did, Rob noticed the ride-alongs were both outside their cars, and quickly moved to get them inside their cars for their own safety. Mark promptly moved to a pickup in front of him for cover. This pickup was parked a mere eighteen feet from the suspect's car and was somewhat parallel to the vehicle with the two in it. This was the same spot where Hagler, while waiting for assistance earlier, had observed the men inside the car. Mark found cover where the cab and bed of the truck join. He positioned himself and unholstered his gun, in the event something unexpected developed. While it can never be known what might happen in these kinds of situations, it certainly seemed highly unlikely that this one would turn deadly, with officers stationed all around the perimeter.

Hagler continued the process of getting the driver out of the car. His commands were loud, clear, and precise. He had remembered one other important thing—he had activated his vest recorder so as to have a recording of the stop. He certainly could not know it then, but the next moments his recorder would catch on tape would be some of the most astonishing seconds of trauma one could bear to hear. He would record an event of sickening sounds and brutal consequences. From that point in time, the tape itself spoke the chilling tale.

Hagler: "Driver." (This is the point when Mark and Rob turned back instead of leaving)

Suspect Driver: "What? Yeah?"

Hagler: "You need to be cooperative with us. Do you understand that?"

Suspect Driver: "If you tell us why we were stopped."

Hagler: "What did you say?"

Suspect Driver: "You tell us why we were stopped."

Hagler: "Okay. When you, when you're changin' lanes, you need to signal for five seconds or one hundred feet."

Suspect Driver: "Oh, come on, now. You know I signaled."

Hagler: "Okay. That's why we stopped you. Now, you need to be cooperative."

Suspect Driver: "You know I signaled."

Hagler: "Okay."

Hagler: "Passenger, I want you to remain in the vehicle, keep your hands where we can see them. Driver, very slowly I want you to step out. Keep your hands where we can see them. Step out of the car."

Suspect Driver: "This sucks!"

Hagler: "You're not under arrest at this time, sir. Okay. Stop right there. Lift your jacket up for me and turn around."

Suspect Driver: "I don't think so!"

Hagler: "Lift your jacket up for me and turn around, sir."

Suspect Driver: "I don't think so!"

Rogers (at driver): "Lift your jacket up and turn around."

Unknown officer: "Get that god-damn jacket up!"

At this point, the passenger starts to get out of the car.

Unknown officer (to passenger): "Get in the car, sir."

Wiggins (to passenger): "Get back in the car."

Unknown officer (to passenger): "Sit down in the car."

Winegar (to suspect driver): "Turn around."

Unknown officer (to suspect driver): "Turn around."

Unknown officer: "Don't move, turn around, hey!"

Hagler: "No! Look out!"

At this moment, a volley of shots began. The driver suddenly pulled a semi-automatic pistol from a holster under his leather coat and began firing. One of his first bullets hit Officer Ron Winegar. The passenger, who already had his door open, exited the car in a crouched position on the passenger side with another semi-automatic pistol firing. His shooting seemed to be cued to what the driver did.

The passenger's first bullet found Officer Mark Stall, who was closest to him, and in the most direct line of fire. Remarkably, by the time he was hit, Mark had already fired several rounds, probably at the driver.

Winegar: "Help, I'm hit."

Hagler: "TAC 18."

Hagler: "We have shots fired. We have officer down."

At this moment, more shots are fired.

Rogers: "Don't! Don't move it."

This statement, "Don't! Don't move it," stirred up a controversy within hours of the shooting. A recording of the shooting was released to the media by the police, along with a transcript. The transcript, because of the lack of clarity without sound-lab enhancement, obviously read according to what the recording sounded like, and what the transcriber understood when going through the tape. The transcript read, "Help! Don't shoot us." Some people would later erroneously assume that this was one of the Brodrick brothers begging the police not to shoot them.

Later, when the FBI worked through the recording with enhancement procedures, they found the actual words to be, "Don't! Don't move it." The voice was Corporal Dale Rogers calling out to Craig Brodrick, who was the driver of the car, not to make another move for his gun, which he repeatedly kept grabbing for when he was wounded and on the ground. Rogers used the word "Don't" four times and the phrase "Don't move it" three times.

After Roger's initial statement, more shots were fired.

Then again Rogers shouted: "Don't move it! Don't move it! Stop! I said, stop! Everybody stop! Everybody stop! Everybody maintain their position right now."

Hagler: "Ron."

Winegar: "I need help."

Hagler: "I know."

Rogers: "Have we got any officers down?"

Unknown voice: "Yes."

Hagler: "Yes, we do."

Rogers: "Get an ambulance now."

Unknown voice: "Yes, two."

Hagler: "Have we got medics en route?"

Rogers: "You call an ambulance."

Van Doren: "TAC 18, we need ambulance to our location. Two officers down."

Rogers: "Now, nobody move."

Hagler: "Jesus Christ!"

Rogers: "Get an ambulance."

Hagler: "We got it coming."

Hagler: "Can I get him outta here?"

Rogers: "Go to him. We got these. Go to him."

Hagler to Winegar: "Where you shot, buddy?"

Winegar: "I don't know, but I need my leg straightened out...my butt..."

Haglar: "Okay."

Winegar: "It's my hip, my pelvis..."

Hagler: "Okay, okay. You're gonna be okay, Ron. Okay."

Winegar: "Okay."

Hagler: "Okay, you're gonna be all right, buddy."

By this time, everyone was frozen in their positions by the command of Dale Rogers to stay put. Disbelief and shock were setting in over what had just gone down. They were also aware that two officers had been hit. Ron Winegar was alive and talking—they could hear him on their vest radios, so that was a positive sign.

The other officer, Mark Stall, was down somewhere behind the pickup parked parallel to the street. Rob Berrier was with him, cradling him in his arms, talking to him, and weeping. What he saw was not good. Mark was slipping away.

5

The Hour of Destiny

Smoke from sixty-two rounds of gunfire was still heavy in the air when additional police units converged at the location of the shooting. In the immediate aftermath of the terrible violence, police radios were buzzing with chaotic shouts and screams from the scene. Code Three responses were coming from every direction—lights and sirens inundated Fifteenth and Idaho.

Officers John Terry and Nick Duggan were among the first post-shooting teams to arrive. They had just taken some juveniles to the downtown substation when they heard gunfire on their vest radios. They went tearing through the heart of the city to the scene. As they jumped from their car, they quickly focused on the scene before them, trying to assess the extent of the mayhem they had heard on their radios. One of the first things they noticed was glittering shell casings all over the ground. Also, they could see activity in several different places around them.

They began moving around, trying to assess what had happened and what could or should be done. They came to Officer Ron Winegar, flat on his back with knees up. He was conscious and had a couple of officers attending to him. He had taken a bullet in the groin, but appeared to not be critically wounded. As they continued further, they could next see two bodies in the area of an older car in the center of the lot. One individual was in a kneeling fetal position, wedged between an open car door and the doorframe. The other was face down on the ground a few feet away, adjacent to the same open door. They were not officers and had likely been gunned down by officers.

Moving still further on the perimeter, they came to Officer Rob Berrier kneeling over someone. As John Terry looked more closely, he saw that it was Mark Stall. His eyes were rolled back and there was no movement or response in his body. When asked where Mark was hit, Rob showed him an entry wound in his right armpit. Rob had already pulled away Mark's uniform, trying to find where he had taken a bullet. Because Terry had seen this kind of wound before, he instantly assessed that there was a "90% likelihood he would not survive."

He stood, and momentarily turned away to try to absorb the shock of what he had just seen. His friend and buddy, sworn into this police department three weeks before him, lay on the ground before him dying. There was nothing he or anyone else could do to reverse this horror. He wept for a few seconds as his emotions overwhelmed him, then flashes of anger surged through him. Somebody, meaning one of the two guys a few feet away, had fired the bullet that had mortally wounded his friend.

Paramedic units were now arriving. Four people were down, two officers and the other two who had occupied the car in the middle of the Rider's Bar lot. The site was rapidly filling with rescue people, off-duty officers, detectives, and bystanders. There was a flurry of movement to find and help the wounded. Three of the four were immediately transported to St. Alphonsus hospital—Officers Stall and Winegar, and the man wedged between the door and frame of the car. Two of the three would be pronounced dead shortly thereafter. The other man on the ground was already dead. Officers involved in the shooting were still trying to shake their initial shock, while those just arriving were greeted by a scene of sickening carnage.

KBCI-Channel 2 television station, located directly across the street from where the shooting took place, immediately mobilized cameras to begin recording the scene in the immediate aftermath of this surreal and aberrant episode. Their footage was the first of what would become extensive coverage of many events related to this shooting. The death of an officer, the first on-duty death in Boise's

104-year police history, overwhelmingly captured the attention of the region, and even extended across the nation. The shootout in Boise became a phenomenon.

The officers who had been part of the shooting were as quickly as possible removed from the location. Non-involved officers and supervisors would deal with what had to be handled on site. Those officers, along with their ride-along passengers, were taken to a local hotel, where they were questioned and debriefed about everything they saw or did. Each was placed in a separate room, and each was individually questioned about what was done. Only Rob Berrier did not go to the hotel right away, because he requested that he be allowed to ride with Mark to the hospital. Another officer, Ted Snyder, also rode in the rescue unit, which was soon screaming toward St. Alphonsus hospital at high speed. Everyone in the ambulance was emotional—they wept while they hovered over their critically wounded friend.

In just a matter of moments, in spite of the high level of activity surrounding the shooting site, the necessity of establishing personal contact with the families of Ron Winegar and Mark Stall came to the fore. Officer Ed Small was dispatched to the Winegar residence to tell Zelphie Winegar, Ron's wife. On the way he picked up Jeff Winegar, brother to Ron and himself a Garden City police officer. Officers John Terry and Nick Duggan remained partners for one more unhappy responsibility—to go to the Stall residence to inform Cheryl Stall about her critically-wounded husband, and get her to the hospital as quickly as possible.

John Terry knew where to go. He had been at the Stalls' now and then, since he worked the same night schedule as Mark. When they were partners, or happened to be nearby, they would stop by to see Cheryl, pick up a quick snack, or down some freshly baked cookies. She was a late-nighter by habit, so their coming by the house at midnight or even later did not bother her. It made the quiet, lonely nights more pleasant and not quite so long.

The two drove to the Stalls' in silence. Their own shock was still very prevalent, since only a half-hour had elapsed since the shooting. As they pulled into the driveway, their hearts were pounding. They knew Mark's situation was perilous, and having to go to the door to tell his wife this kind of news was an impossibly difficult task. But they had no choice in the matter—she needed to know, and she needed to get to the hospital immediately.

They each uttered a quiet prayer and stepped out of the car.

They rang the doorbell. No response. They rang again. Finally, they heard some movement, but the door remained unopened.

Cheryl, startled by the bell, was trying to figure out who was there without opening the door. At first she thought it was neighbor kids, who had been partying late and had managed to keep her awake until a short time before the bell rang. As she peered out the door viewer, she finally saw the uniforms, and opened the door. She assumed Mark was not along, since he would have called ahead to inform her they were coming. Also, Mark always let himself in. Uniforms at her door in this way could only mean something unusual was up. She opened the door, still trying to get herself awake.

"Hey, what's up?" she asked when she saw John and Nick.

Both stood there, unable to speak. Cheryl then asked them in, and they stepped into the kitchen. Again they stood speechless, heads down, arms folded. After a few more awkward seconds of silence, she realized by their body language and ashen faces that something was very wrong. She looked at both, searching for a clue, when fear began surging within her. She instinctively hugged Nick as though to say she had begun sensing their wordless message. They were not prepared for this task; they had not undergone training for knowing the best way to announce to a family what had happened to a loved one while on duty.

Finally it spilled out. "Mark's at St. Al's hospital. He's been shot. He's okay, but we need you to get dressed and go with us to the hospital." The words, "He's okay," were meant to keep her from panic, and to hold her steady.

When one first learns that something abnormal has entered his or her life, it is numbing. You don't know what to do, what to say, or how to make your thinking process react rationally. Cheryl's mind began at that moment processing what she had just heard. She had just been introduced to the unthinkable—to something that would forever alter the course of her life, and leave her never the same again.

She quickly made her way to the bedroom to dress and call her folks who lived five minutes away. It was 2:00 a.m. when she dialed.

Her mother answered, startled awake by the ringing phone. "Mom, I need you to come and stay with the girls. Mark's at the hospital."

"At the hospital? What's wrong? Is he all right?"

"He's been shot, but he's okay."

In stunned haste, Kay and her husband Arnold dressed and rushed to the house. Cheryl's indication that Mark was okay helped restrain their consternation, but their hearts raced as they drove. Upon approaching the house, they saw the familiar sight of a Boise police unit parked in the driveway. Suddenly, the sight of the police car that morning sent a surge of fear through them, as they realized Cheryl had not received a phone call about Mark, but had been informed by officers who were at her house.

Kay remained with the girls, who were asleep. Cheryl jumped into the blue and white with Nick, while John Terry rode with Arnold. They followed the patrol car so closely that Arnold ran at least one red light trying to stay with them. John Terry chided him to ease up, they would get there fine. Fortunately, the streets were quite empty.

But Terry was himself nervous. His thoughts were verbalized in the course of this ten-minute trip to Saint Alphonsus Hospital. He expressed that he was tired of losing buddies. He'd already lost two when he worked in LA, and he had enough of that for a lifetime. A chill went down Arnold's spine. John Terry was preparing him by divulging the seriousness of this situation—Mark's survival was apparently in question.

Nick drove Cheryl close to the emergency entrance. Arnold and John parked further out in the lot, which put them a minute behind. Inside the entrance were clusters of people—officers in and out of uniform, medical people, and who knows whom else. A nearby emergency room door was open, and inside was a frenzy of activity and voices. Though that door was open, it was screened off. Cheryl couldn't be positive, but she felt sure Mark was in that room.

A senior officer suddenly realized that Cheryl was present. He said to nearby officers, "You need to get her out of here. She would be better not to be here."

Just then, John and Arnold came in. A gesture by an officer just inside the door, meant for John Terry's eye, also caught Arnold's attention. He moved his head side to side in a slight nod. It was another unwelcome indication that Mark's situation was not looking good.

Cheryl and Arnold were escorted to a small waiting room away from the hub of activity. Several people followed, asking if they could help in any way or get anything for them. Don Peterman, Police Chaplain, introduced himself and led in prayer, then stepped out of the room. His gentle manner momentarily helped calm swirling emotions.

As they waited, Cheryl asked for an outside line to call Mark's parents in Cupertino, California. After several glitches, including nervously dialing the wrong number, she finally got through. Mark's mother, Nancy, answered.

As soon as she heard Cheryl's voice, she said, "Cheryl, what's wrong?" She instinctively knew something had to be wrong, for the hour was too late for any other kind of call.

"Mark's been shot...." That's all Nancy heard as she screamed and dropped the phone.

Nancy's sister, Joyce was staying at the Stall home that night because Ray, Nancy's husband, had gone to a men's retreat over the weekend. After a lapse of some seconds, and after realizing that Nancy had just been given some kind of shocking news, Joyce came to the phone. Cheryl informed her that little was known about Mark's condition, and that she would call again when she knew more.

The minutes that followed were agonizingly long and filled with anxiety. A myriad of thoughts ran through the minds of a 29-year-old wife and her father as both sat, prayed, and paced. They kept asking themselves, "Is this really happening? Could it actually be true that we are in process of losing our Mark? If he doesn't make it, what are we facing? Surely, surely this is not so!"

At times likes these, one's mind and emotions blur together in surreal imaginings; all that is supposedly happening lies beyond reality, so it seems. A silent process of rationalization began: "Mark has to live. He is too special, too honorable, too needed by so many, too young to die. Oh, Lord, no. Please let him live; let him come back to his family."

Meanwhile, Kay Rubey had called her sister with news of the shooting. She in turn called another sister, and they began spreading the word among local family members. None knew how serious this actually was, since little information was available.

Officer Dan Warren, a day officer in the Selective Traffic Enforcement Program (S.T.E.P.), was taking an additional shift at the downtown substation this particular night. He had talked to Mark earlier that evening, when he and other officers were in for a foosball game at the station. Warren, a veteran of the Boise Police Department and a member of the same church as the Stalls, soon realized it was his friend Mark who had been wounded. He immediately called his wife, who in turned called the point person for the Lake Hazel Baptist Church's prayer chain. At 2:30 a.m. phones began ringing throughout homes in the congregation.

Nothing was known about the circumstances of the shooting by the family up to this point. No one was asking, and right then it didn't matter. What mattered first and foremost was that Mark Stall somehow survive.

Finally, Lynette Townsend, a Boise Police wife and also a nurse, could stand it no longer. "I'm going to go check and see what's going on," she told Cheryl. When she returned a few moments later, she reluctantly whispered, "It doesn't look good."

Surges of emotional panic again accelerated. This is not the way this should be coming down. "Lord, this is Mark Stall. He's one of Yours. Surely, You are not willing that he be taken from this life only to leave his family husbandless and fatherless. Lord, please, not this."

The jumble of pleading thoughts was starkly interrupted by Dr. Stephanie Bodes' entrance into the crowded waiting room. She knelt before Cheryl and tenderly took her hands in her own.

"I'm so sorry," she said, "but Mark did not make it. We did everything in our power to pull him through, but the damage was just too great for him to overcome. I'm so sorry we could not save him."

She paused as the impact of this devastating news began to set in. For a few moments, total helplessness gripped everyone. Nothing more of meaning could be said, and nothing more by way of help could be extended. Dr. Bodes finally said, "When we get him cleaned up and prepared, you can see him if you wish."

In that overpowering moment, the world, as this family knew it, stopped. For Cheryl Stall and family, the ember of hope which had been burning faintly, was now extinguished. The most horrible of all words that mortals can hear about someone they love, had just been uttered. Mark Stall, 29 years and 10 months old, no longer possessed life. His earthly journey had come to an end. He had passed into the ages.

Arnold took his daughter into his arms, and together they cried. Neither could speak for a few moments. They wordlessly began absorbing the overwhelming pathos that now exploded in their hearts. There was only one thing they could do—weep, and release some of their overflowing sorrow. What lay ahead in the next moments, hours, days, and weeks—would soon enough demand they find a shoreline, somewhere, somehow, that would keep them from sinking in this ocean of grief.

The time was 3:00 a.m., September 20, 1997—a date of infamy for this family and for a community. Boise could no longer be quite the same, or as innocent. It had just surrendered a prized citizen, a guardian of its peace, to the ultimate sacrifice. A man in blue had died on the streets of their city, doing what they hired him to do—protect them. They were still safe, but he was not.

Mark Stall had fallen in the line of duty.

6

We've Lost Mark

Cheryl Stall and Arnold Rubey, though immediate family, were not alone in grief. Everyone in the corridors of the emergency wing of the hospital was impacted. Officers, even the most seasoned, were now overcome by uncontrollable emotions. Their fraternal world, their brotherhood, their law enforcement family had just suffered an irrevocable loss. The sadness associated with this tragedy was spreading; no one easily remained outside its clutches.

After a few moments of trying to assimilate the shock of Mark's death, Arnold picked up the waiting room phone to call Kay, who was at the Stall house waiting and wondering. He dreaded making this call, because she was likely alone and would be crushed emotionally.

"Hi," he said weakly.

"Hi. How's it going? How's Mark?"

He paused, then stammered, "Not very good. We've...we've lost Mark."

She started to respond with another thought, when the impact of what she had just heard hit her. "What did you say?" she asked. She thought she had not accurately heard him.

"We've lost Mark. He didn't make it."

She voice turned shrill and loud. "We've lost Mark? Oh, no! We can't have lost Mark!"

Then came a few seconds of awkwardness, then a moan of tears. She finally blurted out, "What am I going to do? I've got Nancy holding on the other line. She called here a few minutes ago to get the hospital phone number, and I was still talking to her when you called. I asked her to hold because I assumed this might be news about Mark. What am I going to tell her? I can't tell her this. What am I going to do?"

"You've got to tell her," he responded. "There isn't any other choice."

He ended the call feeling disoriented and helpless. His wife had just been unavoidably put in the position of not only being alone when hearing of the loss of her son-in-law, but also forced to break this devastating news to Mark's mother. It would be one of the worst things a mother could ever hear—that her son is dead. How will Nancy handle this? Will Kay be okay with having to do this?

Kay waited for a moment as she tried to get a grip on her rampant emotions. She was already in shock, feeling disbelief and grief, but knew she nonetheless had to collect herself before getting back with Nancy. After several agonizing moments went by, she realized there was no easy way to break this news, even if she had had ample time to prepare.

Just do it, she told herself.

She got back on the line. "Nancy, that was Arnie calling from the hospital. Did you say someone was there with you? Did you say your sister Joyce is there?"

"Oh, no!" Nancy screamed. Kay never finished telling her. Nancy dropped the phone.

As earlier, when Cheryl first told Nancy of the shooting, her sister had to step in and pick up the conversation. Tragically, the latest word was the worst—Mark was gone. Joyce now bore the responsibility of being the point person to pass this shocking news to the rest of the Stall family. The grief-stricken Nancy could not perform the needed task just then, for her life as she knew it had just collapsed.

Matt Stall, Mark's older and only brother, was immediately called and told of his brother's death. He rushed out of his house into the black night and walked the neighborhood, trying to handle the calamitous news he had received. Matt and Mark, though six years apart in age, were close; they were good buds. Matt had not only lost a brother, but his special friend. His world had just come unglued.

Matt had little time to be alone with his grief. He had to assume another responsibility—that of telling his father. Ray Stall had gone earlier that Friday to Camp Hammer for a men's retreat. The camp location was three hours away in the Santa Cruz Mountains. Matt's sister Louise and her husband Charlie Malone lived nearby, so he and Charlie decided they would go together to tell Ray that his youngest child was dead.

They had an additional concern. Ray had developed serious heart problems a few months earlier, and had been hospitalized because of his condition. Mark had taken work leave during that time, and driven with Cheryl to California to be with his dad and the family. It would be the last time all the Ray Stall family would be together.

When Matt and Charlie arrived at Camp Hammer, it was 5:00 a.m. in California and still dark. They had no idea where to find Ray, so they went from room to room trying to locate him. After disturbing several rooms of sleeping men, they found him and roused him.

"Oh, you decided to come after all, huh?" Ray groggily murmured.

"No, Dad," Matt whispered, "that's not why we're here. We've come to tell you that Mark has been shot."

"Is he going to be okay?"

"No, Dad, he didn't make it."

As Ray lay back on his bed in pained shock, Matt laid his head on his dad's chest, and they cried together.

After Kay was off the phone with Joyce, she felt overwhelmed with grief and helplessness. Thankfully, her sister Gayle and her husband Jeff Nelson arrived within a few minutes. Officer Dan Warren met his wife at the hospital, drove directly to Cheryl's house, and arrived shortly thereafter. The Nelsons then remained with the girls while the Warrens drove Kay to the hospital.

In a short while, word was sent that Mark could be seen. Cheryl's father again asked her if she really wanted to do this. She nodded—yes, she wanted to see him. He then placed his arm around her as they began their pained and tearful trek to where Mark's body lay. This walk seemed agonizingly long, as if it were in slow motion.

As they moved through the corridors, a remarkable scene unfolded before them. The hallways were lined on both sides with dozens of grieving officers and friends, side by side in wrenching homage to their fallen brother. Later, they both recalled how stupendous this sight really was—people watching them, crying, and striving to hold up for them. However, it was impossible to remain untouched in this black hour of grief.

When the door opened and they stepped in, they could see no evidence of the frenzied activity that had taken place not too long ago in this very room. It was now fully in order, cleaned and prepared for this visit. This was in marked contrast to what one officer had experienced just a short time earlier. Hesitatingly, he told them that during the time Mark was being frantically worked on, he had been posted just outside the room and had had to stare at a footprint in Mark's blood outside the door. Mark was his friend, and this was almost more than he could bear.

Mark lay directly before them at the back of the room, his feet toward them. White sheets covered his body up to his neck, and both arms lay outside the sheeting, with his hands folded together at his waist. His face showed no signs of stress. His hair was neat, as always. His head was tilted slightly to his left.

The door closed behind them. A nurse remained.

Both Cheryl and Arnold were taken aback by his peaceful appearance—they had expected evidence of his ordeal to be reflected in his face. It was not. Rather, it was as though he had calmly climbed into the bed where he now lay and closed his eyes for a peaceful rest.

While there was no visible evidence of the damage done to his body, he had sustained massive internal damage from a single 40mm bullet that had entered his right chest at the armpit. That bullet severed a pulmonary artery not much larger than a pencil lead. It was a perfect shot with respect to guaranteeing death. Even if his wound had been received in the hospital, where he would have had immediate care, it is unlikely that he could have been saved, due to unstoppable bleeding. Although his initial blood pressure readings appeared to show rather positive indications, these were misleading. Even though his blood was pumping at a strong rate, it was all going into his chest because of the severed artery.

The bullet was halted in its path by the backside of his ballistic vest, and lodged against his spine. It was later learned that had Mark survived, he probably would have had significant spinal problems, including the likelihood of being a quadriplegic. For him, the ultra-active guy, that would have been a living death.

As they moved to his side, Cheryl reached out and tenderly placed one hand on both of his, and placed the other on his head. She then leaned over to hug and kiss the face she knew and loved. Her tears spilled on his lifeless body, while she whispered her love to him. Arnold stood behind her, sobbing and holding on to her as though she were about to fall. Their tears just could not be stopped at a time like this.

They stayed but a few moments, silently gazing on the form of the beloved one who would never again speak or come home. For Cheryl, it was almost impossible to believe that she had talked to him a mere three hours earlier, and now she would never talk to him again. Finally Arnold urged her toward the door, as much for his sake as hers. The pain he felt from watching his daughter say good-bye to her husband was rending his heart.

Later, Cheryl expressed how glad she was to be able to see and say good-bye to Mark in that room in that way. In the beautiful casket that would later hold his body, it would not be the same.

As they finally moved to the door, the attending nurse hugged Cheryl, and through her own tears said, "I'm so sorry." She represented the untold numbers of people who took this sorrow personally and became immersed themselves in the lamentable circumstances of Mark's death.

As they exited the room, many of those who had lined the corridors outside when they entered were still there. They had respectfully remained and waited. Expressions of sorrow and sadness were spoken by some; others could say nothing.

As they made their way back to the waiting area to decide what to do next, Arnold was struck by the sight of at least five couples from Lake Hazel Church standing in the corridors. Each couple had chosen to come to the hospital to await word on Mark. Without hesitation, when they received word about his shooting from the church prayer chain, they had abandoned their night's sleep and headed to the hospital.

This small but caring church would be gripped, then and later, by a deep grief. They had just lost a respected member of their family, a young man they loved and cherished. Mark and Cheryl had become a special part of their lives and their friendships, and the shock of knowing he was gone was starkly etched in their faces.

By this time Kay had arrived at the hospital and was waiting for Cheryl and Arnold to come out of Mark's room. They all three huddled together and cried. In a few moments, they returned to the waiting room to decide what to do next. As they sat and talked, Cheryl was approached and asked about organ donations. It was a delicate task to inquire about such a thing at such an awkward time, but immediate permission was necessary if it was to be an option. Did she have a preference or desire about this?

Cheryl's husband had barely been pronounced dead, and already she faced a very emotional decision regarding his body. What would Mark want? She thought for a moment, then agreed that Mark's organs could be used as needed. She signed the necessary forms, and Mark's death was already in progress toward helping someone in need.

Police Chief Larry Paulson had by this time arrived at the hospital, and was keenly feeling the trauma of losing one of his officers. His countenance was suffused with the pain of this loss. He had borne the load of all the previous incidents in which lives were lost at the hands of his police department, but this was very different—he had now had one of his own needlessly taken. On his watch as commander in chief a great many things had happened, and in not one respect did he have the slightest choice about the circumstances of each incident. While he was surrounded with friends, supporters, and fellow law enforcement people during this trying time, it was still lonely. No one could really know how great his burden was.

He expressed his sympathies to Cheryl and the family, and assured her that his department would stand beside her to help in every way possible. That promise was kept. Chief Paulson saw to it that Cheryl Stall and her girls were looked after during the days, weeks, and months that followed.

There was no longer any reason to remain at the hospital. It was decided that Cheryl and Kay would go back to the Stall home, and that Arnold and others who wished would go to the police station for a scheduled 4:30 a.m. briefing. Chief Paulson would conduct that briefing with known information regarding the shooting.

An officer drove them to the station, which was located only a couple of miles from the hospital. An eerie stillness was in the air, and darkness was still deep when they drove into the back parking lot of the police complex. As they drove down the aisle closest to the entry, Arnold spotted Mark's car, parked there a mere seven hours earlier. Mark, of course, had fully expected to get into that car and drive home at the end of his shift. The sight of the Oldsmobile, sitting and waiting for its owner, formed yet another of many emotional elements that were part of this tragedy. He wept as they drove within a few feet of the car.

The briefing was scheduled for the station auditorium. As people trickled into the large room, each, without exception, entered somberly and then sat in stunned silence. What could be said? What words were fitting? The silence alone was emotionally overwhelming. Occasional whispers were exchanged, but no one had words to speak at such a time.

Four-thirty came and passed. The chief was not ready. Word was then sent that it would be 5:00, and the wait grew even more excruciating. Arnold finally asked an officer friend next to him, "What's going through your mind right now? How is this affecting you?" It was unfair to ask such a question at a time like this; however, the officer responded with sobering words.

"Every day that I go to work for the next ten to fifteen years, my wife will worry about whether I will come home again."

Arnold was speechless. This officer had precisely identified the most graphic concern any law enforcement family could have. In the aftermath of a tragedy like this, families all over this city and nearby regions would enter a new level of actuality. It was later learned that one officer in a smaller community immediately quit his position and moved out of state. A future ombudsman candidate for the city of Boise was in the process of hiring on with the Boise police department when Mark's death occurred. She immediately withdrew from going further as a policeman.

An officer losing his life on the job in Boise was no longer just a possibility—it was a reality. A policeman, someone they knew, a friend— had within these last few hours laid down his life in the very city in which they worked. The impact hit home big-time.

What would now keep any of them from packing it in? Why would they want to stay in a profession in which the risks increase rather than diminish? What would spouses feel in the hours and days ahead? How would their children respond to the sudden death of someone who does just what their daddy does?

Finally the chief entered the room, walked to a small podium, and began presenting sketchy details of what was known and suitable for public release. There were two "suspects," as he called them, who fired semi-automatic pistols at police officers after a routine traffic stop. Both were dead. They were identified as Craig

Brodrick, 29, and Doug Brodrick, 27, of Brush Valley, Pennsylvania. The name of the fallen officer would not yet be released.

As the chief finished his briefing and fielded a few questions, his frustration vented. "I'm mad," he said. "I'm damn mad." With that, he quickly left the room, followed by the room's occupants, all soon to greet the dawn of a day none wanted to face under such bitter circumstances.

7

Flashbacks

The Chief was not alone in his anger. Boise's men in blue knew it was inevitable that this sort of tragedy would happen in the city. Sooner or later, one of them would go down, for the community was growing too large, too fast to realistically escape a fatality within the ranks. Yet no one could mentally or emotionally prepare for such a thing, and now that it had become a reality, a surge of sheer reactionary passion about the crass killing of an officer gripped the entire law enforcement family.

This particular situation was so senseless, so frustrating, so repugnant in every way: a good man's life was snuffed out due to totally absurd behavior, and the two men responsible for Mark's death also foolishly forfeited their own lives in the process. That they set themselves up for destruction with their reckless resolve to shoot it out was mind-boggling. Everybody lost and nobody won. The good and bad alike were blotted out that morning.

Now attention was focused on the young officer who had courageously laid down his life in the parking lot of a biker bar. Family and friends now faced the task of looking back over Mark Stall's life in a myriad of ways they would not otherwise be compelled to consider.

His life, as are most people's lives, was a normal one, with most of what he was and did as a person simply the process of basic everyday living. He certainly was not famous, nor was he widely known in the community. Undoubtedly, he was not appreciated by some citizens or even acquaintances; but that would now change. Mark Stall, the man and the officer, would now become well known—looked at closely for who he was and idolized for laying down his life. Strangers and acquaintances alike would now see him in new ways.

Reflection on a person's life after death often takes curious twists—things are weighed in ways both true and exaggerated. In some cases, like this irrational killing, the first emotion to surface is anger. It may begin with animosity toward God. "If God is so gracious and loving, how could He allow this? What did I ever do to Him to deserve this kind of treatment? Why would He take someone away who is so honorable? And why in the prime of his life?"

God, to angry survivors and close friends, could readily become the prime object of blame. After all, He is the Sovereign who could have prevented death, but didn't. The logical conclusion to this way of thinking is that we have every right to be put out at God. He is roundly resented for not having prevented cruelty.

There can also be, and often is, an intense anger toward those humanly responsible for causing the death of a loved one. Particularly in the aftermath of death caused by foolhardy behavior, animosity and spite toward the perpetrator(s) readily surface. A drunk driver kills innocent people; a worker causes someone else's death through carelessness; evil people with deliberate intent snuff out an innocent person's life to satisfy their own wicked desires.

It is becoming more and more common for law-breakers to defy, threaten, injure, or even kill law enforcers who get in their way or hinder their plans. These kinds of death naturally draw reactions from affected family members, who are left to deal for a lifetime with the emotional consequences of someone else's deadly actions. They have had their loved one stolen from them because of the foolishness of irresponsible people, and they are totally helpless to do anything about it other than grieve.

Still another sense of anger may be directed at the one who died. This mystifying reaction follows reasoning such as, "Why did he have to go and die on me? How could he do this and leave me all alone to deal with what's left? He had no right to leave me (us) here in what is now going to be a miserable life with all its problems." This reaction usually does not linger long, because the reactionary anger soon turns to sadness.

An opposite emotion may also surface. The one taken in death is almost instantly viewed as having had few or no faults; he or she is reverently elevated to the surreal status of having been a flawless saint. This kind of response sometimes assuages the guilt or tensions which have been carried over from unresolved conflicts. Survivors yearn for everything to be okay, since resolution is no longer an option; therefore, the deceased person becomes more saintly in death than he or she was in life. Rose-colored glasses replace reality.

One other significant feeling often arises from the loss of a loved one: the one lost is compassionately mourned because of having been vulnerable and helpless before the insensitive enemy named death. Survivors feel great sadness because of their loved one's inability to retain life; therefore, because of this sadness, unsavory memories are disregarded. The lost loved one is looked upon with different eyes, even if he was a scoundrel.

Family members, friends, and acquaintances of Mark Stall had to individually deal with each of these reactions in respect to his life and death. Each had to sort out who Mark really was to them in life, and how he should be viewed in death. Would Mark be made bigger in death than he really was in life? Would there be severe anger and spite over this mindless murder?

The hours and days ahead challenged every family member in regard to how they would deal with their individual grief, and how they would deal with Mark's memory. The most important issue would be to put forth Mark's legacy as it should be, without distorting reality. To his credit, his manner of life made accolades and kudos easy. He was an honor to his parents, and he was loved by his immediate family, friends, and brothers in blue. He certainly was not perfect, but he was an honest, straightforward man of integrity. In short, he was a man of whom family and community could truly be proud.

Recalling highlights of his mostly ordinary life did unveil some distinctive events that had shaped what he became. He was distinctive at birth—ten and a half pounds worth! At age four, he underwent exploratory surgery at the Stanford Medical Center for lingering sicknesses, but nothing serious was ever found, and he grew to be healthy and strong.

One major incident during his teen years changed the direction his life would take. It headed him in the direction of the vocation that would ultimately cost him his life.

In June 1984, at age sixteen, he had just completed his junior year in high school and was enjoying his first "real job" at a Baskin Robbins ice cream parlor in Cupertino, California.

One evening that June, Mark stopped by the store where he worked to get some ice cream. A school buddy and neighbor, Steve Letchworth, was working that particular evening and was just ending his shift when Mark dropped in. Steve was without transportation, and since he lived only a few houses down the street from the Stalls, Mark offered him a ride home.

They drove home in Mark's 1970 Datsun pickup. Mark parked on the street in front of Steve's house, and both got out of the pickup to talk. Shortly, a man neither knew approached them and asked if they could provide a match for his cigarette. "No," Mark said, "but I can get you a light from my pickup lighter." He opened the door and pushed in the lighter. When he looked up, the barrel of a gun was in his face.

"Get in," the stranger said. "We're going for a ride." He forced both boys at gunpoint into the pickup, and ordered Mark to start driving. Since it was about 10:30, darkness had settled over the city.

They drove aimlessly for some time, and then the man ordered them into the hills above Palo Alto. When they came to a remote area, the stranger told Mark to park, then ordered both boys out of the vehicle and made them strip. They were then told to put their clothes in the bed of the pickup and get back into the cab. Mark was moving to the other side as instructed when Steve decided their risk was too great to do nothing. Since he was near the gunman, he grabbed the pistol and yelled for Mark.

Mark dashed around the pickup and also grabbed at the gun, already held by four hands. The semi-automatic pistol discharged, putting a bullet through Steve's knee. In spite of his injury, Steve continued to struggle for control of the gun, as did Mark. Then the weapon jammed. The kidnapper panicked and ran off into the darkness. The boys quickly pulled on their clothes, though Steve was by now really feeling the pain from his wound. Mark flipped on the headlights of the truck to try to spot the keys, which had been fallen into the dirt when he went to help Steve. They also feared the return of their abductor. Fortunately, they found the keys quickly and headed out of the hills to find a phone and call the police.

They came to a cluster of houses, and Mark jumped out and knocked on the door of the first house. There was no answer. He went to the next house and got the same non-response. People were naturally afraid to open their doors at midnight, and besides, some of them had heard the shot echo through the night moments earlier.

Finally, he pulled Steve out of the pickup and laid him on someone's lawn. He began calling out to anyone in nearby houses to call the police—he had a friend who had been shot and needed help. Finally, someone—without opening a door—placed a call. In a matter of moments, police and paramedics arrived. Steve was immediately transported to the Stanford Medical Center, while Mark stayed with the officers to return to the scene of the crime and help reconstruct their abduction.

It took almost a year to capture their abductor. At age twenty-seven, he already had a long record and had been out of jail for only a few months during the last ten years of his life. At the time of the kidnapping, he was on parole in Nevada. He had stolen his father's pistol, which he left behind at the scene and which led to his eventual arrest and conviction. He was given a fifty-four-year prison sentence for this crime.

Mark was impressed by how the police handled his and Steve's ordeal, and as a result began to seriously consider law enforcement as a potential career. He liked their spirit and helpfulness, and decided he wanted to be like the helpful police who had cared for Steve and him. He would like to serve people with integrity and concern, as they had.

After Mark's death, Cindi Gil-Blanco of the Palo Alto Police Department wrote the Stall family about her memories of Mark.

"I was one of the first officers," she wrote, "from Palo Alto Police to respond up to the foothills to the home where Mark and his friend sought safety that night in 1984. Although I never saw the boys again, what struck me was the bravery and courage shown by Mark. It would live in my memory for a very long time.

"I always thought that if I had a boy (which now I do), that he would have his head on right, like Mark, and that I could instill those characteristics in my son that you obviously did with Mark. I'm sure that Mark had many opportunities as a police officer to touch other people's lives (as a cop), but way before he put on that badge, he touched mine."

Memories of another sort also surfaced during these early stages of coping with Mark's death. One had to do with his matriculation at The Master's College, where he picked up work on campus in paint maintenance. Mark, as would be expected, quickly learned the ropes and grew into a skilled and knowledgeable painter. He would later use what he learned during those two years to supplement his income while in law enforcement. He earned a reputation as a perfectionist in his work and an expert in the know-how of painting. In his four short years in Boise, his skill at his side-work of painting, wallpapering, and refinishing decks became well known and appreciated.

The most graphic memory, however, to haunt the new widow was the recurring dream Mark kept having. That very afternoon—the day preceding his death—he again dreamed the same dream. He brought it up again to Cheryl just hours earlier when he had awakened from sleep in preparation for that night's shift. What he repeatedly experienced in that dream not only now terrified her, but left her unable to escape the sensation of fear it must have brought to him. She shuddered every time she thought about it.

Mark envisioned a scenario in which he was shot while on duty. Over and over, in every dream, he experienced taking a bullet. Even more distressing was the end result of this bullet—death; it was always fatal! He periodically mentioned this dream to Cheryl, not to scare her, but to let her know the repetition and restlessness he kept having over this morbid nightmare. He assured her there was nothing to it in reality; but now that "nothing-to-it" dream had actually come to pass. She was now overwhelmed by the thought of this terrible premonitory vision, particularly for Mark, who had dreamed about taking the shot that killed him only scant hours before he actually took it. In reality, he then experienced his own dreamed-of demise! Thinking upon this was, for Cheryl and those who learned of it, unbelievably stunning.

Mark's legacy was already being shaped in the minds of his family and his many friends. His mother-in-law, Kay Rubey, said of him, "He was bigger than life." He was not easily forgotten once one became acquainted with him. His winsome smile, crowfoot lines radiating from the outside corner of each eye, and wispy voice made him distinctive. Though he was a bundle of energy, and tended to make some people nervous because of his energy, he was likeable and a pleasure to be around.

One trademark was his talk—at times, much talk! Those who endured his lectures after being stopped knew he could talk, usually much more than they appreciated. Yet he was kind and considerate, and did not needlessly belittle anyone. He had a way with certain people and certain kinds of situations, which enabled him to defuse further problems. He worked at being sensitive and helpful rather than just street-hard and callous. He was truly a caring cop.

Co-workers knew he loved practical jokes. He was often part of pranks at the station on fellow officers, and was often the one who came up with innovative ideas or ways to pull off what was desired. While he could dish it out, he could also take it. This balance in his disposition gave him a thumbs-up with friends.

All that was now over. Mark's presence was gone. No part of him, other than memory, would any longer exist. Thankfully, there were many special memories to bless his family and friends over the coming years.

One very special thing occurred ten days before his death. Mark and Cheryl's older girl, Jonelle, celebrated her sixth birthday on September 10. Whenever the girls had a birthday, or during special holidays, it was an occasion for a big celebration. Mark would get out the camcorder and capture the event on tape. Usually he was the one behind the camera, and so was seldom included in the pictures that were taken.

On this occasion, however, things were done differently. Buddy and Janice Jacob with their four girls, and the Rubeys, were part of Jo's party. Buddy, a fellow officer and friend, told Mark he would be the cameraman that night so that Mark could be part of the filmed festivities. As a result, throughout the evening, Buddy filmed the family enjoying this special occasion. Most important of all, as it turned out, was the fact that Mark was included in most of the filming. He was extensively recorded showing Jo how to ride her new bike, doing the barbecue which he always enjoyed providing, and helping Jo enjoy her special day in several other ways.

Buddy Jacob filmed an evening precious beyond imagining that night. It was vintage Mark—enjoying his girls and making the evening special for them. That video will always be a priceless treasure and a cherished memory to Cheryl and her girls. It was ordained on this occasion that Mark would leave a visual record before his unexpected and untimely departure from this life.

8

A Widow and Two Children

When daylight broke, word was rapidly spreading throughout the Treasure Valley that a gun-battle had erupted in downtown Boise during the night and that at least one police officer was dead. The printed and electronic media were well underway at putting together the first of dozens of stories to evolve from this tragic event. In the meanwhile, stunned family members began to converge on the Stall home. In a couple of cases, the shock was so grievous they could not bring themselves to face Cheryl or the girls until they could come to grips with their own brokenness. Family away from the area began processing what to do about coming to Boise for a funeral. Most would come. They had to be there for Mark's sake— and for Cheryl's.

The most painful task at the Stall home was the impossible one of breaking the news to two young girls that their daddy would not be coming home again. The numbness that the young widow and her parents now felt clouded their senses as to how to handle such a delicate process. It was too overwhelming a sorrow to even think about. Ultimately, as their mother, it fell to Cheryl to determine how it should be done.

The concern over telling them had several considerations, the main one being the deep love they had for their daddy. Jonelle, barely six and Julia 3 1/2, idolized Mark and always cherished their moments with him. Their fun-filled evening mere hours before when playing Freeze and dancing around the house, would still be fresh in their memories. When they would awaken, they would find they no longer had a daddy. How would their young minds assimilate such news? What would this do to them now and later, even years later?

Both girls awakened around 8:00 a.m. As they sleepily exited their rooms, they were surprised to hear voices, then to find people throughout the house. They quietly and curiously wandered around trying to figure out what was going on. They looked for their mom, but didn't see or hear her anywhere. She had earlier been taken to her bedroom to lie down, and was being kept company by her mother. Someone finally saw the girls and knocked on Cheryl's bedroom door to inform her that the girls were up. She took a moment to prepare herself, then went out to them. They could tell she had been crying. She immediately took them into her bedroom, where her parents joined her to help in this stressful task. They closed the door, after which Cheryl placed one girl on each side of her on the bed as she knelt before them.

In preparation, she had placed a framed picture of Mark on the bed. It was a familiar portrait to the girls, but they didn't think anything of it as they sat down on the bed in front of their mother.

She paused for a few seconds, then slowly and softly spoke. "Whenever you want to talk to your daddy..." She halted for a moment, fighting her emotions, then continued, "...you can pick up this picture and talk to him."

She could go no further. Tears surged down her cheeks. The girls stared at her, confused by her crying. "What's wrong, Mommy? Why are you crying?" they asked. Their startled faces were glued to hers.

She struggled to regain the ability to talk. Finally she found the strength to continue. "Last night some bad people shot your daddy, and Jesus took him to heaven. He won't be able to be here with you anymore, but you will always have this picture to remind you of how much he loved you."

All three adults were now sobbing uncontrollably. Jonelle and Julia, stunned by the raw pathos before them, broke into their own kind of unnatural, shocked cry. They did not yet fully grasp what they had been told, but they knew this was terribly bad by the way their mommy and grandparents were weeping. They had never watched a scene like this—grown people, whom they knew very well, feverishly sobbing. The raging emotions they were witnessing drew from them a distorted wail that in and of itself was strange to the ear.

For several minutes they all cried, unable to talk. Both girls snuggled to their mother and held her close, then all five of them huddled together and shared their sorrow. After some moments, Jonelle reached down and brought her daddy's portrait a few inches from her face, staring at him through her tears. It was the first of many times to come that she and her sister would look at that familiar face, only to know they would never have or hold him in the flesh again. Hereafter, he would only be a memory. His face and arms, felt in pleasure and security only twelve hours earlier, could never again be known this side of heaven. They had just been forced into carrying on their lives without him.

Jonelle and Julia, at the tender ages of six and three-and-a-half, would now experience that the security of having their daddy with them as they grew up was not to be. To them he was invincible, able to overcome all things and do all things, just because he was *their* daddy. Now they had just been informed that the man they called "the strongest man in the world" was gone, which meant he was vincible after all. He had fallen at the hands of unthinking people who callously intended to kill any or all of the officers they faced, and did indeed succeed in killing one—these two little girls' precious daddy. It was a senseless act of cruel and vicious behavior.

As the girls began processing the sad, unreal news of their daddy's death, things began to intensify around the house. The Stall phone, though unlisted, began to ring steadily, soon necessitating the addition of a second line. Officers began coming to the house for various tasks related to the aftermath of the tragedy, which caused the phone situation to intensify. Those with cell phones had to press them into service as well.

The Boise Police Department began a watch at the Stall house that would continue as long as it was considered necessary. Within hours after Mark's death, it was determined that at least one uniformed officer would be at or near the premises at all times. A police car would always be visible in front of the house.

By late Saturday morning it was evident that several officers were needed to care for the myriad of details that were rapidly unfolding. One officer was needed in the house just to cover phone calls and screen the people coming to the premises. So many people began appearing that family members themselves ended up being screened before being allowed into the house. The officers did not know them, of course, and Cheryl was emotionally unable to watch for and greet those who were showing up.

As the hours wore on, it became natural that the Stall residence would become the center of operations between the department and the family. This would continue until after the funeral. Neighbors accommodated the turmoil of this hectic time with graciousness. They had to put up with constant traffic, people milling through the neighborhood, and the continuous hubbub of voices and activity. At times, they even had difficulty exiting their driveways because of the crunch of cars.

By mid-morning, Cheryl wanted to get out of the house and walk—somewhere, anywhere. Not wanting her go alone, Arnold went with her. They had walked less than a block when three Garden City police officers passed them on their way to Cheryl's home, all friends of Mark. They recognized Cheryl and stopped, sorrow evident in their faces and voices. They awkwardly expressed what they were feeling, struggling to say what they hoped would be the right words. Finally, they stated they had something to give her, and she asked if they would mind taking it to the house and giving it to her mother. They agreed, and when invited in, they stood crying. Cheryl's mother later shared how deeply she had been moved to see these tough officers weep so tenderly. They had lost a friend and fellow officer, though he was from another police department. They showed the depth of their brotherhood by providing a check from their department in the amount of $500.00 for Cheryl and her girls.

Mark's parents, Ray and Nancy Stall, along with two of their other three children, Matt and Louise, found seats on a Saturday afternoon flight from San Jose, California. The Boise police department arranged transportation for them from the airport, but it was wisely decided that someone familiar should greet them along with the uniforms of Mark's fellow policemen. Arnold said he would be willing to be there for their arrival.

The contingent sent to greet the Stalls gathered in concourse B. While they waited, Arnold was introduced to Corporal Harry Kindelberger, a veteran motorcycle officer in the Boise department.

Harry would be an integral person in the transportation require-ments of arranging the funeral. He worked tirelessly to put together one of the most memorable events in Boise history. His expertise in the traffic aspects of special events, including police funerals, was well known in the northwest; but until this time, he was never needed to work one within his own department. He had never wanted to, of course, but he was now required to work at home for a fellow brother. It was very bitter for him personally, as well as for the entire department.

As would be expected, the Stalls were in shock from grief when they stepped into the concourse. They were glad to see Arnold's familiar face, but his presence being surrounded by several uni-forms drove home the dark reality that Mark had indeed died. They, like others who have lost a loved one in sudden death, formulate subconscious thoughts that just maybe this was not real after all, that they can shake themselves or awaken from this nightmare and see their loved one again. Not so. Not now. Not ever. This death hap-pened.

Arnold's grief also confirmed that they were coming to Boise to bury their son and their brother. They wordlessly but emotionally embraced. No words in those first moments could adequately express the pain they all felt. The Stalls were then transported to Mark's home, where they would greet their daughter-in-law and granddaughters for the first time without their son being there along with his family. They could scarcely picture in their minds what this would be like. Their ride through Boise was a blur; anything and everything around them meant nothing. Their boy, their brother, meant the most of all. His absence made Boise on this day into a city they did not want to see.

That afternoon, Mayor Brent Coles phoned Cheryl to express his personal condolences and as a representative of the city. She appre-ciated his call, despite the fact that at that time the Boise police department was six months overdue for a contract settlement with the city. Mark was not a member of the union, but all law enforce-ment personnel benefited by the terms of the union contract. Those facts aside, the Mayor's call heartened her. He asked if he might be permitted to come to her home that evening to meet the family, and she said yes.

The Boise City Council likewise extended sympathy to Cheryl and the Stall family by providing flowers delivered by Sarah Baker, a council member who may have felt some awkwardness under the circumstances. The law enforcement community generally felt that the Council was reluctant to show supportive appreciation for their police department, nor did they seem to realize the worth of the sacrifices that officers often made in the performance of their duties. Now, as a Council, they had to face the grieving family of a young officer who literally gave his life protecting the city that they represented and served. It was a delicate situation for Sarah, the Council, and for Cheryl as a widow. Nevertheless, it was gracious of Sarah Baker to come.

By late afternoon, one of the pressing questions was who would do the funeral. Cheryl and Kay both asked Arnold what his thoughts were. Did he want to conduct the service himself? If so, could he realistically handle the responsibility of it? Everyone knew that this would be an extremely emotional event, and it obviously would not be good to have him breaking down and be unable to finish.

They were also aware of another factor: Arnold's father, Peter Rubey, had passed away only two and a half months earlier, and Arnold had conducted that funeral, which was very difficult for him. Perhaps this was too soon for him to be involved in the funeral of another close relative, especially one whose death was as sudden and shocking as Mark's.

There were still other considerations. Mark had loved and respected his grandpa Rubey and wanted so much to be at his funeral that he had taken planned vacation time to drive Kay, Cheryl, and himself to Colorado to join Arnold, who was already there because of his father's impending death. Mark did not want to miss this last link to the memory of his grandparents, since his grandmother Rubey had passed away a year earlier and he had been unable to be at her funeral. Arnold had also conducted his mother's funeral, and the family knew he was still carrying emotional baggage from these deaths.

While he had managed to handle both funerals satisfactorily, this one was very different—the unique circumstances of this death made the task even more difficult. Mark was young and filled with vitality, and now he was needlessly gone because of senseless violence. His death had created an emotional trauma that was unlike anything they had ever experienced. The question was, could and would this family handle these circumstances in a noble way, or would they be reduced to weakness and overwhelming sadness?

Was Arnold even close to being up to this task?

With little hesitation, Arnold said yes, he wanted to do the funeral. He wanted this final opportunity to honor Mark as a son. He well knew, however, that he would have to completely trust God to get him through the service, for it was impossible to not feel inadequate in the face of such a task.

One further personal reason was a part of Arnold's wish to lead Mark's service. He and Mark had become good friends, growing closer as the years passed. He and Kay had watched Mark mature during the last third of his life even more than his parents, because he had lived during those years away from them and his boyhood roots. He and Cheryl had lived close to the Rubeys for most of their post-teen years because of college and their marriage. Ray and Nancy had raised a fine and honorable son whom the Rubeys had had the privilege of watching first-hand as he matured. Mark had some growing yet to do in some areas, but had made significant strides in others.

As a son-in-law, Mark had had to adapt to his in-laws, as had they to him. Could they, would they get along well? Mark was sensitive about this part of family life, and worked hard at being a respectful, helpful person in their lives. He was a delight to be around, and to Arnold he had become more than simply a son-in-law—he had become a close, younger friend. Because of this, Arnold wanted to do one last thing for Mark—a very special thing—he wanted to conduct his funeral as a personal valediction to a beloved son. Mark's parents and family also desired to be part of providing a special and personal farewell to their loved one.

As evening approached, food began arriving in abundance. As family and friends began to arrive in Boise, gracious and thoughtful people throughout the community responded by providing not only food, but other kinds of giving as well. Their hearts were open and generous.

That evening, Mayor Coles and Chief Paulson came to the Stall house. The Mayor stepped into the living room, where family members and others were crowded into all available spaces. As he spoke to them, he wept. That he was deeply affected by the tragedy was clearly evident. He assured Cheryl of his personal support as well as the continued support of the community for her and the girls. When he finished speaking, Cheryl shared with him that she was being carried by God's grace. She expressed that she could not understand why she had to be a widow and why her girls had to grow up without their daddy, but even so she just wanted God to be glorified through it all.

After listening to several family members speak about how they were handling this tragedy, Mayor Coles moved around the room embracing every family member. That evening would be the first of numerous times he would express his support with an embrace. He then stepped into Cheryl's kitchen, where he stood alone for a few moments. He looked forlorn as he scanned the simple surroundings of their home.

Chief Paulson then shared how grieved he was over losing Mark. His burden was heavy, and he could not know how this family might respond to him or his department under such bitter circumstances. However, he and his entire force of officers would find complete support and appreciation from the family. Without hesitation, Larry Paulson reached out to them in every possible way, and provided support for them as their burden of grief grew.

Finally, as this first night drew toward its end, detectives Dave Smith and Greg Morgan came to the house to brief the family on what they had learned about the shooting. They were two of the main detectives on the case, and had already spent many hours trying to sort out the details.

Dave Smith spoke first, but became so emotional after a few words that he could not continue. Greg Morgan picked up at that point, and provided a somber overview of what they knew. The two who had fired on the police were brothers from Pennsylvania. One of them had been in the area only a few months, the other less than two months. They had been pulled over for a routine traffic violation, but were then observed to be acting suspiciously after the stop while they remained in their car. Because of this, backup had been requested, and Mark and his partner Rob Berrier were among those who responded to the request. Preliminary findings showed that dozens of rounds of ammunition had been fired at the scene. Also, a search of their Boise apartment revealed that they possessed a stash of weaponry, including bomb-making manuals. There would be continued investigations into the brothers, of course, but this was what was known less than twenty-four hours after the shooting.

The detectives made themselves available whenever any of the family wanted their help or requested information that they were free to share. Everyone was horrified by what they had just heard, and worn out by what they themselves had experienced in a few short hours. Now they faced the first night when they would all go to bed knowing that Mark was gone.

Sleep proved to be fitful or elusive for all concerned; for many it would be hours yet before they could rest. Several watched their bedroom clocks tick toward 1:20 a.m. When that moment came, they shuddered and cried in the darkness, knowing that exactly twenty-four hours earlier, Mark had taken the bullet that took him from them. They tried to imagine what it must have been like, and found the thought utterly devastating.

It was, however, only the beginning of sorrow. Much more would follow.

9

Funeral Preparations

At daybreak on Sunday, thirty hours after the shooting, Cheryl was very sick. She began throwing up and could do nothing but lie in bed in misery. Her terrible burden was now even worse—not only was she feeling the horror of having just lost her husband, she was now also physically ill. In a way, she just wanted to die. Deep inside she knew there would eventually be a life ahead for her; that she would one day be able to anchor into a new life filled with new hope. At this point, however, her world had unraveled, and held little meaning other than that she knew God was there, and that He had not made a mistake. Her bewilderment was deeply felt, of course, but her faith was still stronger than her despair. Also, she had two precious girls who desperately needed her, and needed her whole. Right now, however, she was utterly and completely miserable.

Arnold awakened, after a night made restless by wondering what to do about the Lake Hazel congregation. He had little heart for even going to church, to say nothing of leading a service, yet he sensed he needed to be there. Also important to the church was the fact that Mark and Cheryl had become a special part of the church community—they were loved as a couple, along with their two girls. On this day, this congregation would be broken and grieving, and would need some kind of encouragement to help heal their shock over losing Mark.

Arnold finally decided to have a time of sharing and prayer, to whatever degree he and they could stand. Kay remained with Cheryl, and Arnold drove the nine miles to the church alone. On the way he stopped to purchase a Sunday newspaper. He did not intend to read it then, or perhaps not even any time soon, but he wanted it available for when the time would be better.

As he entered the store, bundles of the *Idaho Statesman* newspaper lay stacked before him. Mark's picture jumped out at him on the front page. He was taken aback by the sight of that picture—it was a shocking reminder that death had actually claimed Mark. He decided to pick up three copies, and walked to the counter with tears coursing down his cheeks. The clerk stared at him. He muttered something about the sadness of what was on the front page, but she was unresponsive, and said nothing in return.

When he arrived at the church, a few people were already there, milling around in a daze. No one seemed to be talking, and none knew what to say to him. Everyone and everything felt awkward; all were struggling with the painful circumstances. Ray and Nancy Stall, despite their grief, decided to participate in this service, hoping to draw whatever strength they could from the fellowship and the people.

The unstructured service turned into an incredibly moving and emotional hour, devoted to talking about Mark and the sufficiency of God's grace in spite of the terrible heartache. When it concluded, everyone had in an unusual way experienced a strengthening—they knew God had graciously met with them and helped them. The balance of the day's scheduled activities and services were canceled; the people had no heart to do more.

By Sunday afternoon, the pressure was building to formulate specific funeral plans. Detective Alan Hardwick, a good friend of Mark's, asked what the family had in mind for a funeral location. Arnold said that their little church building would probably be inadequate, an assessment they would later laugh about. His total miscalculation of how big an event this funeral would turn out to be was brought to reality when Alan said that the Boise State University Pavilion might be the right size. Arnold was incredulous. "You've got to be kidding—the Pavilion? No way!"

Alan went on to explain. "You don't understand—this is going to be a huge funeral. Law enforcement officers from many places, including several states, will be here, along with their police cars. Also, the community response is expected to be tremendous. A very large facility will be necessary to accommodate the crowd and the traffic."

The next question was on what date to schedule the funeral. The sooner the better would be easiest on the family, but they now realized that they had to be flexible about this because of the inordinate amount of preparation required. They finally settled on Wednesday, September 24. The logistics of putting together an event of this magnitude were especially demanding on the police department and the Pavilion staff.

The Department became the intermediary between the Stall family and all who needed information, wanted interviews, or required the addressing of a myriad of other details. Arnold tried to protect Cheryl as much as possible from having to deal with anything other than the most important details. Other family members took on whatever responsibilities they could. As pressures and tensions evolved, everyone seemed to be protecting someone else. As a result, the processes of communication became complex and difficult at times. It was the only way, however, to survive the constant onslaught of activity.

By Sunday afternoon, the Stall residence was wall-to-wall with people and activity. Food continued to pour in until there was literally no place to put it. A neighbor had two additional refrigerators delivered from his appliance business and set them up in Cheryl's garage. Campers and motor homes were provided for incoming family, and area motels made available upwards of fifty donated rooms, as needed. Police wives, friends of the family, and church people readily made themselves available for whatever needed to be done. So many people did so much during this time that it would be impossible to adequately recognize or compensate their selfless sacrifices and commitment of time. The family itself had no comprehension of how much was being done for them.

An inquiry had been made as to whether the Stall family would be open to a television interview that Sunday afternoon. The family discussed it, then agreed they should and would do something publicly. Television reporters had been at Lake Hazel church that morning and had conducted brief interviews with a few family members. The first full interview, however, occurred at Summerwind Park in northwest Boise. Lane Lyon, KBTV's reporter, brought home to the

Boise community for the first time what Mark Stall's parents and family were really like.

While preparations were underway for the interview, Gary, the cameraman, told Ray Stall that he knew Ray's son. He proceeded to tell the story of how he was late to work one day and pushing hard to get there quickly, on top of which he was very stressed out. Mark had stopped him for speeding, which prompted Gary to give Mark a "song-and-dance" story of pity, to which Mark patiently listened. Then Mark told Gary to knock it off, because things really weren't as bad as he was making them out to be. Mark calmed him down, and urged him to relax and take it easy. Gary told Ray that Mark's manner of handling him had actually uplifted him, in spite of being given a ticket. Later, Mark and Gary even cultivated a friendship, and occasionally had coffee together.

The interview came off okay, but going through it was hard. Cheryl, who was feeling better by this time, came to the interview, though she refused to go on camera. Everyone was in deep shock, and trying to cope with new adjustments with every hour that went by. The long-term emotional darkness of Mark's death was just setting in, and would actually worsen later on when things began to slowly quiet down.

Mayor Coles called Cheryl earlier that afternoon to tell her that she and her family had given him the courage to do something he needed to do. He would be holding a 6:00 p.m. news conference that evening to address the community about this tragedy. At that conference, he decried the savage actions of those responsible for Mark's death; he praised the Stall family for their family unity; and he addressed wounded officer Ron Winegar and his family with hopes for a full and speedy recovery. He petitioned the community to support their police department, and to calculate at what cost law enforcement people do their job.

Appealing to the community to attend the funeral with their families, he ordered City Hall closed so its employees could attend, and requested that businesses and government agencies do likewise. Flags were ordered to fly at half-staff throughout the city.

Finally, he boldly stated, "This may not be politically correct, but this lack of respect, this flaunting of authority, is the root of the problem…" (that of Boise police being involved in shootings in the past two years)…individuals have refused to follow the direction of a police officer." He also affirmed his complete faith and confidence in

Police Chief Larry Paulson. The family did not hear the conference, because of the intensity of so many things going on, but they appreciated his boldness when they read his remarks later. (See the complete text of Mayor Coles's press conference in the Appendix).

On Monday morning, fifty-five hours after Mark's shooting, Cheryl, Ray and Matt Stall, and Arnold Rubey drove with Officers Harry Kindelberger and Rich Fuhriman to Dry Creek Cemetery north of Boise to select a grave plot. Dry Creek came highly recommended, and it also would better accommodate the lengthy procession that would come to the cemetery following the service at the Pavilion.

As they walked to the Eagleview Section at the north end of the cemetery, they became very emotional. "This is ludicrous. Why are we doing this? It just isn't possible that we are at this cemetery for the purpose of picking a grave site for Mark. He can't be gone." The site finally selected by Cheryl provided a remarkable setting for the graveside part of the funeral forty-eight hours later. Everyone walked off the hill in silence and sadness. It was just the beginning, however, of another long day full of painful experiences.

Next was a visit to Alden-Waggoner Funeral Home in Boise to select a casket, so Mark could be readied for viewing by the family that evening. Steve Gordon, Tim Alden, and their fine staff helped bridge the way for a memorable funeral with tireless preparations. Their part of handling Mark's funeral was carried out with finesse and dignity. Before the family now, however, lay the task of selecting a casket. It was the second major emotional event that morning.

While all this was going on, Mark's brother Matt and brother-in-law Charlie Malone decided it would be fitting to erect a cross at the site of Mark's shooting. They opened the phone book and randomly selected Anvil Iron Works in Meridian. The owner, Ed Schmitt, a former Nevada sheriff's deputy, said he would be honored to take care of their request. He immediately constructed the cross with iron crosspieces, painted them white, and then donated it to the family. Matt and Charlie took it to Fifteenth and Idaho in downtown Boise and placed it in the ground, in a strip of weeds and stickers between the sidewalk and Idaho Street. A few hours later, the weed patch was replaced with sod, making the area more attractive. Little did they or anyone else know that the placing of this simple cross would develop into a controversy two days later (see Chapter Twelve).

Prior to the placement of the cross, but even more so afterwards, people began visiting the site to pay their respects. Many left flowers, cards, notes, candy, teddy bears, and what-have-you. At times the cross was surrounded with heaps of beautiful flowers. Officers periodically collected the notes and cards and brought them to the family. For a short period of time in Boise, Fifteenth and Idaho became a shrine.

On Monday afternoon, Ray Stall and Arnold Rubey met at the Boise State Pavilion with pavilion staff, police representatives, TV personnel, and others necessary to the planning and carrying out of the funeral. The decision had been made to request use of the Pavilion, and the University graciously provided their facility for this purpose. Upwards of thirty people met for three hours to work through the details.

With Monday evening came the difficult emotional experience for the family of the viewing of Mark's body. Up until that time only Cheryl and Arnold had seen him, when they viewed his body in the hospital after he was pronounced dead. This would be extremely difficult for each person to go through, and was dreaded by everyone.

Cheryl asked to go first, taking with her the girls, and requesting that they go alone. Opinions varied as to the wisdom of allowing the girls to see their daddy in this way, but Cheryl had thought this through and felt that the pros outweighed the cons. She believed that for the girls to see their daddy would help them more readily grasp the reality of his death, and that it would enable them to better understand his absence in their lives. No matter what, this was an incredibly emotional and unpleasant experience. Nothing felt right about any of it.

She readied the girls with pretty dresses and beautifully braided hair. They were so cute and prim that it seemed reprehensible to have to defile their innocence with what they were about to encounter. Arnold stood outside the room but could observe them as they slowly made their way to the casket. He wept as he watched them stand and look upon Mark's body. The grief he felt for these three precious people was suffocating. Cheryl quietly and extensively talked to the girls about their daddy, after which she allowed each of them to touch his hands and face. They instantly knew that this was not their daddy in the way they used to know him. By doing this, they now knew he really was gone from them.

His countenance was not what they remembered. For one thing, unknown to them, their daddy's eyes were already implanted in two other people's bodies. Some of his skin and bones had also been utilized to help others. The cold, harsh feel of his lifeless body was in stark contrast to his warm arms about them in life. After a short while, they walked away from the casket bathed in tears. Julia later begged to be allowed to go back in to see her daddy again, and cried all evening over not being allowed to go back. Once was already one time too many, though.

Next, one by one, the family quietly and somberly entered the viewing room from the side entrance, to see Mark laid out in his police uniform. When Nancy finally entered, though she was thirty feet from the casket and could barely see Mark's form, she gasped and had to grab a nearby chair to sit down. What does a mother feel at a moment like this? What is felt about the one to whom you have given birth; the one loved and nurtured in every way when he could not care for himself in tender youth; the one who joyfully and pleasingly graced your home. She was now utterly helpless to aid her son. No one can quite know what Nancy Stall felt in that room on that night.

When everyone had returned to Cheryl's home after the viewing, another emotional experience awaited them. Detectives Dave Smith and Greg Morgan had again made themselves available for questions and information. After they had shared a few more details about the case and were about to leave, they were asked to explain more precisely how the shooting had happened. No one in the family had been watching the news or reading the papers to any extent, as it was just too painful, so the additional details about the shooting were unknown to almost all of them.

The detectives informed the family that they had with them a copy of Officer Bryan Hagler's tape recording of the shooting, which would give them the actual sounds of how events unfolded. The recording was not very clear, and they had only a small tape player to play it in, but they would make it available for the family to hear if they wished. After a moment of discussion it, the consensus was yes, they wanted to hear the tape.

All of the more immediate family who wished to listen gathered in a downstairs bedroom. A dozen people crammed themselves into the small room by sitting on the floor or the bed or by standing. Greg Morgan then turned on the tape. Bryan Hagler could be heard beginning his move to get the driver out of the car. The exchanges between Hagler and the driver could be heard, not distinctly, but clearly enough to get the drift of where things were headed. Then was heard, "No, look out!" and the sound of gunshots pealed out of the recorder. The crisp sound of semi-automatic weapons being fired caused Linda, Mark's oldest sister, to burst into a loud, involuntary wail. She and everyone in that room knew that one of those sounds was the bullet that had killed their loved one. To hear a recording of that morning's actual death scene was overpowering.

For a few moments no words were spoken; only the sounds of weeping filled the room. There was nothing to say; it could only be felt. The tearful silence continued, then someone began to sing a hymn. After a while, someone prayed, then others did likewise. The prayers were a release to the pain that all were feeling, and the long day's events came to an end that night in that room.

On Tuesday morning, Cheryl was deeply depressed. She could not get out of bed; she could only weep out of despair. Emotionally devastated and desperately grieving over Mark's passing, she struggled with fears that she would never again feel happiness in the way she had known it before. She was so down that Kay asked Arnold to join her in Cheryl's bedroom, to be with her and try to provide some comfort. For a long while, all three talked, wept, hugged, and prayed. They had no recourse but to ask God to provide consolation for their broken hearts.

This day would turn out to be another very busy one. It was now only twenty-four hours before the funeral. The entire day had been set aside at Alden-Waggoner Mortuary for public viewing, beginning at 9:00 a.m. The line was continuous throughout the day, as hundreds of people paid their respects to Mark and the Boise Police Department by stopping by. One couple, former neighbors of Mark and Cheryl, were so distraught over Mark's death that they came to the mortuary twice that day.

On this Tuesday morning, a news reporter who had respectfully requested an interview with Matt Stall, again asked for that opportunity. He finally felt the time was right, and asked that she meet him at the mortuary that morning. When she arrived at the appointed time, he asked her to follow him.

"Where are we going?" she asked.

"To see my brother," he said.

"I'd rather not do that," she replied.

Matt was insistent. "You said you wanted to do an interview. This is going to be part of the interview."

She reluctantly went with him. She hesitated when they came to the viewing room, but Matt nudged her towards Mark's open casket.

"Touch him," he said.

"I don't want to touch him," she replied, now emotionally upset.

Matt took her hand and placed it on Mark's lifeless hand. She immediately pulled away, repulsed by what Matt had done. "You said you wanted to know what it felt like for me to lose my brother, and what it is like to go through this. Now you know a little bit more about what it's like."

By this time it was becoming critical that Arnold begin to get ready for his responsibilities the next day. He literally had not had time since Mark's death to even think about, much less prepare what he might say at the funeral. In desperation he asked two out-of-state friends to represent him and the family at a final walk-through meeting at the Pavilion on Tuesday afternoon. John Zimmer, a pastor friend from Washington state, had been sent to Boise along with his wife by his church leaders, to be present as long as necessary for their friends, and Mick Pagach literally put his job on the line in California to be there for and through the funeral. Both men were of significant help in pulling things together with respect to the family's wishes about what would and would not be acceptable. The placement of television cameras and the taking of still pictures were some of the concerns they worked through with the police and the media.

Arnold finally escaped to his church office, where his secretary shielded him as best she could from interruptions. Even his church office worked against his ability to concentrate, for another reason. Mark had remodeled this office for him a year earlier, and looking at the surroundings only crushed Arnold's spirit more. In fear and trepidation, he tried to quiet his raging emotions and collect himself so he could begin formulating his thoughts. He cried out to God for the wisdom and strength to do what he knew he could not begin to do on his own. He was so emotionally broken that he felt he had been little help to anyone else up to this point; how he was going to speak at his son-in-law's funeral under such conditions? It was beginning to appear unlikely that he would actually be able to perform the service he had committed to, but it was too late for change. He had to pull himself together.

For three hours he struggled and strained. At the end of those hours, God had given him the message he felt led to speak. Furthermore, he now had peace that all would be well. He went home and confidently told Cheryl and Kay that it was going to be all right—he felt ready for the day to come. That he felt positive regarding the coming day was a great comfort to them, because up to this time they had been worried about his ability to go through with it successfully.

On Tuesday night at the Pavilion, the very location of Mark's funeral the next day, a Christian concert by Clay Crosse was held. Mark and Cheryl, along with several other couples, had planned for many weeks to attend this event together, then return to the Stalls for refreshments afterwards. Instead, as it turned out, Clay Crosse dedicated his concert to the memory of Officer Mark Stall, and Mark's friends attended his funeral.

10

A Day Never to be Forgotten

Wednesday, September 24, 1997, the day everyone dreaded—the family, the police, and the community. The day of a funeral is always hard on a family, any family, and for this entire household to have to deal with the necessity of burying a vivacious man like Mark was incomprehensible. To go through this was like gazing up at the top of a formidable mountain from its base and knowing you had no choice but to scale its looming elevation. Although the task seemed impossible and would be treacherous the whole way, the mountain had to be climbed and conquered.

The magnitude of what was coming had been building up over the past four days. It was clear by now that it was going to be a huge and emotional event, one that would be etched in most everyone's memory for a lifetime. When it was over and being recorded as written history, most of those closely connected with the funeral found themselves without adequate words to describe what they had experienced. It lay beyond their ability to verbalize because only in reality could its impact be fathomed.

The family began to gather at Cheryl's home at 8:00 a.m. They were scattered in many places around the city, and there could be no slip-ups in having things ready when the time came to go. Every available limousine in the area and every available car among family members would be needed in order to transport over one hundred twenty people from the Stall home. The Pavilion had set aside seating for one hundred forty-four family members and designated friends.

The day was expected to be warm, as high as eighty-two degrees, and already the heat was being felt, though it was yet early morning. Overhead an air balloon hovered in the region of the family gathering, likely with cameras on board to film the gathering and procession.

At 8:30 the roar of motorcycles down the street drew everyone's attention. Wave after wave of police motorcycles entered the area and were set up to lead the procession from the neighborhood to the Pavilion. Each was manned by a uniformed officer. The sight and sounds of those powerful machines was the first of many awesome sights that would send chills down everyone's spine that day.

The plan was to transport everyone at the Stall residence to the Pavilion in a procession. First they would go by the mortuary, where the hearse bearing Mark's body would join them, then to the Boise Police Station for one final stop for Mark, and finally to the Pavilion.

The procession began at 9:00 a.m. One by one the cars pulled out of the neighborhood, forming a very long train of vehicles. It took several minutes to reach Alden-Waggoner Funeral Chapel, where they paused only long enough to allow the hearse bearing Mark's body to enter the procession. That vehicle was directly in front of the first family car, which carried Cheryl and her two girls, the Ray Stalls, and the Arnold Rubeys. Officer Buddy Jacob, a family friend, drove this car. Other family members, pallbearers, and close friends followed in succeeding cars.

Most of those in the procession assumed that the reason for driving by the police station was simply due to protocol, but all the officers knew the true purpose and dreaded what it symbolized. When the entourage was a couple of blocks from the station, Buddy Jacob suddenly gasped from emotion, as the impact of the entire proceedings hit him hard. Arnold, who occupied the front seat with Buddy and was unaware of how emotional the final call would be, reached over and took Buddy's white-gloved hand into his own as they glanced at each other with tears welling in their eyes.

They rode silently until the hearse stopped directly in front of the station on Barrister Drive. Some of the officers who were driving the first few family cars raised their mobile phones high enough so that all in their cars could hear the numbingly emotional final call.

"Boise 489," said the voice of Officer Harry Kindelberger.

"489," came the acknowledgment.

"Be advised that Officer Stall is ten-nineteen." (present at the station)

"Copy."

Then came the cryptic tone-alert to all officers.

"All units stand by," called Dispatcher Linda Lyons. "This is the final call for Officer Mark Stall, Ada 512."

"Mark, you'll be deeply missed."

"All channels will now observe a twenty-second moment of silence in remembrance of Officer Mark Stall."

Twenty-seven seconds later the last words were spoken. "Final ten-forty-two (end of watch) at 0924 hours."

The entire call took just over a minute, and was powerfully moving. Muffled emotions overtook all who were privy to the sober meaning of Mark's final call. Perhaps at no other time during the entire ordeal was the word "final" more deeply felt. Words could not and would not be spoken for many minutes following this experience.

When the final call was complete, the processional immediately restarted and moved toward the Pavilion, five miles away. Upon arrival, they were greeted by a sea of police vehicles—bumper to bumper, row upon row, covering acres of parking alongside the BSU stadium. The sight of all those cars, vans, and trucks was simply staggering. The count of police vehicles ranged from six hundred to one thousand, representing at least seven states in addition to Idaho, and each car carried from one to four officers.

The procession halted momentarily while photographers and media people were moved out of the way as the family vehicles entered the area reserved for them. They then parked and entered a waiting room inside the arena. Refreshments were provided as they awaited the beginning of the service, which was now only minutes away from its scheduled start.

Blue ribbons were distributed at the entrances to demonstrate support for the men and women in blue who would and do give their lives in service to others. The five thousand ribbons that had been prepared ran out long before the service began. The community responded to the call to attend, and many families brought their children. All wanted to be part of this extraordinary event to honor a fallen policeman and those who live and serve like him.

Finally, it was time to seat the family. They quietly filed out of the large room where they had gathered, to rows of seats reserved for them on floor level directly in front of the platform. As they entered the huge auditorium, the sight of the massive crowd before them was overwhelming. With the exception of the designated family chairs and those in which the Boise police would shortly be seated, the entire floor level and the next two levels all the way around the arena were filled. The crowd rose to their feet as the family slowly and somberly filed in. Musical selections, chosen by the Stall family for the funeral, were playing over the arena sound system as they entered.

On the platform were Boise Mayor Brent Coles, Police Chief and Mrs. Larry Paulson; David Maddox, who had performed a part of Mark and Cheryl's wedding eight years earlier; Bill Herman, who organized and conducted the music portion of the funeral; Dee Sarton of KBTV, who sang; Jill Odom, who played the piano at Mark and Cheryl's wedding; Detective Alan Hardwick of the Boise Police Department, and Arnold Rubey, Mark's father-in-law.

Eight officers, all good friends to Mark and representing five different police and sheriff's departments in Idaho and California, served as pallbearers. The City of Boise Police Pipes and Drums and the Boise Highlanders piped and drummed their unique and mournful sounds, as Mark's flag-draped casket was brought through Entrance Four and slowly carried to the front.

Arnold Rubey began the service by stating that a great sorrow had touched the souls of a family, the Boise Police Department, and a community. He ended the introductory segment by stating, "It is now time to stand en masse, shoulder to shoulder, rank after rank, in grateful tribute to the dedicated, brave men and women who are in the trenches for us. And because this is so, I would ask you out of your sorrow today to say so."

The audience stood and gave a lengthy applause in honor of law enforcement personnel, whose worthiness was rightly and proudly acknowledged that day.

Mayor Coles' remarks included the announcement that the City Council was committed to naming a future Boise park in Mark's memory. Chief Paulson stated that he disliked being the chief when one of his officers went down, but was honored to have Mark Stall as one of his officers, and was honored to be there on that day.

Officer John Terry, who some weeks earlier had been presented the Medal of Valor for his bravery in a fatal incident months earlier, spoke plainly about how evil had intended "to kill the uniform and star that night, but it got Mark instead." He further described being at the scene that morning, then going to Cheryl's home to tell her Mark had been shot. Officer Terry closed his remarks with a very moving and selfless gesture. He reached into his pocket for the medal he had been awarded and said, "To Mark Stall, who faced grave personal danger, I am giving you my medal." He descended the platform steps to Mark's casket and placed his medal on Mark's portrait, which rested on top of the bier. The audience rose to its feet in acknowledgment of his act of honor to Mark, and broke into applause that was by then mingled with tears.

Detective Alan Hardwick spoke of Mark's faith in God and his love for his girls, and stressed that Mark had died a true hero, trying to protect his brother officers.

Mark's two sisters, Louise Malone and Linda Olsen, and his brother Matt, all shared recollections of Mark's life, followed by Ray Stall speaking in honor of his son's life. Their remarks included humorous anecdotes, which helped lift some of the cloud of sadness that hovered over this day.

David Maddox, a Los Angeles pastor and friend to Mark and Cheryl, read from Mark's Bible some selected passages that had had held much meaning to him. Dee Sarton and Bill Herman sang "More Than Wonderful," a favorite song of both Cheryl and Mark. The Boise Highlanders and the City of Boise Pipes and Drums presented the very moving "Highland Cathedral."

Arnold then presented the message he had struggled to put together the day before. The funeral was already nearly two hours in length when he began to speak, but this particular time in the service was the focal point of what really mattered about Mark Stall's death. He spoke to the issue of dying, and about being prepared for eternity. Thankfully, Mark was prepared, and Arnold could say with confidence, "I know where Mark is. He is at home in heaven, where he had made prior preparations."

He continued, "I look upon you many law enforcement people in this audience today. It moves me beyond description to see you here in this setting and in this way. We all honor and salute you and rightly so. But I ask you now a question of greater importance than what your uniform represents, your code, your commitment to justice—

were it you rather than Mark, would you have been ready? Do you know now that you are ready?

"I likewise look upon the balance of this vast audience, and I ask, are you ready for eternity? The importance of eternal matters exceeds the value of your business or your earthly commitments; it is greater than your possessions or your treasures here. It is the biggest issue of all."

The service ended with Julie Heinrich singing a stirring rendition of, "We Shall Behold Him." Julie had wept through the entire funeral until it came time for her to sing. She then used her beautiful voice to emotionally and fittingly conclude an unforgettable memorial service. Everyone present in the Pavilion, and also those watching via television, were reminded of God's grace and promises to mortals who were prepared.

The impact and emotion of this service, felt so deeply by so many, were so powerful at its conclusion that Gerry May, KBTV's anchor, could not speak on air for several minutes. His emotional struggle was a fitting reflection of the feelings of those who were present at the funeral. His co-anchor, Carolyn Holley, bravely carried on until Gerry could finally speak.

Within minutes after the service the procession of police vehicles began moving toward Dry Creek Cemetery in northwest Boise. The hearse and the family were to come at the end rather than the beginning. When the family finally did leave the Pavilion, the first cars had just reached the cemetery—a distance of ten miles!

Moments after the funeral ended, while the family awaited their time to leave, Arnold saw John Terry standing alone in an area under the Pavilion complex. He stood with shoulders stooped and head bowed, deep in thought. Arnold approached him in tears and embraced him. He managed to say to John, "You are one special man. What a selfless act on your part."

"No," said John firmly. "Mark is the one who deserves it. He earned it."

When the hearse and family finally left the Pavilion and pulled onto Broadway Avenue in Boise, they were astonished to see people lining both sides of the streets. As they drove into the heart of Boise, the crowds increased—mile after mile, they lined the streets. School children with signs and hands over their hearts; grown men and women with tears streaming down their cheeks; men standing at attention or saluting. They lined the streets the entire distance to the cemetery. It was one of the most astounding sights and sensations anyone in the Stall family had ever experienced, or ever would. And it was all for their precious son, brother, husband, dad, cousin, and friend. They were completely overwhelmed by this expression of support.

Midway to the cemetery, as everyone rode quietly and with a sense of awe at what they were witnessing, Nancy Stall broke the silence. "You know," she said, "if that was not my son in that car ahead of us, he would be calling home tonight and saying, `Mom, you'll never believe what we saw today.' Mark was always impressed by big and well-done things. This would have impressed him."

The entourage drove through two huge ladder-trucks parked on Gary Lane to demonstrate the support and camaraderie of the Boise Fire Department. This impressive sight left another indelible impression.

When the hearse and family cars finally reached the cemetery, one of the girls desperately needed a restroom. A small restroom within the cemetery complex was located near where they had entered, so the procession was halted for three minutes to accommodate the need. Then they slowly proceeded another quarter of a mile through the heart of Dry Creek, behind a riderless horse.

At the gravesite, three awesome things commanded attention: dozens of motorcycles in formation down an adjacent road; hundreds of parked police cars glimmering in the sunlight in a field adjacent to the burial site; and two lines of officers forming a passageway to the crest of the hill where Mark would be buried. Surrounding them were hundreds of other people.

It was hot, and many of these officers had stood for quite a long time in the blazing sun. As the pallbearers struggled up the incline with the casket, the pipers played "Amazing Grace" one more time. Arnold spoke a few remarks, the flag was folded and presented to Cheryl, taps echoed across the hillside, and the riderless horse struck the familiar "End Of The Trail" pose. The funeral was over.

All across the hillside, people fell into one another's arms and sobbed. Emotions exploded. Both seasoned officers and normally unemotional men wept unabashedly. Many were so overcome that they could not speak. Those assembled had said their final goodbye to a special friend, who did not belong on this hill to which he had been brought. His glistening casket formed the unwelcome center-piece of this gathering. It was a very hard goodbye.

11

A Community Touched

The response to the Stall funeral clearly showed that the moral nerve of the entire Boise region had been touched. They did not view Mark's passing as just another ordinary death, even though he was a stranger to most of them. Instead, corporately they felt a tremendous loss—an honorable officer had been needlessly slain while confronting the evil that lurked in their community. They were jolted to the core by the terrible cost paid by a man who stood in harm's way to protect their city. People everywhere were moved by his sacrifice and wanted to do something to show their support.

Along with estimates of up to three thousand officers, thousands of other citizens attended the funeral, and additional thousands lined the streets of Boise to watch the procession pass before them. Many thousands more watched on television. Even those who were unable to participate in any way in the funeral were still moved by news articles and telecasts about Mark Stall and his family.

Finally, there was the factor of live television coverage of the funeral throughout the entire northwest. One woman shared that she and others were glued to a television set showing the funeral as they exercised in a Seattle health club six hundred miles away—they could not take their eyes and ears away from the emotional service. Four nights later, KBTV Channel 7 in Boise rebroadcast the entire funeral in prime time. Elsewhere in America where reports of this police shooting were provided, people were strangely moved by the story coming out of Boise, Idaho. They were curious about the young family that had experienced such a loss.

One result of all the coverage of the tragedy was the desire it evoked in people to do something to show support; they wanted to respond tangibly to the family. One such individual was Jack Lawford, who owned and operated Jack's Stereo Shop in Boise. Jack had developed a friendship with Mark as a result of the stops Mark made at his shop on patrol, which led to his patronizing Jack's business occasionally for personal car-stereo needs. Mark always loved good electronics, though he usually couldn't afford to indulge the level of his tastes.

On the fateful Friday night and Saturday morning of Mark's death, Jack had been riding his new Harley Davidson motorcycle around Boise searching for his officer friend. He knew Mark was probably on duty that night and had decided he would to try to find him so he could show him his new bike. He knew Mark would appreciate the magnificent machine. However, he was unable to locate him and finally gave up the search.

Jack was devastated when he heard about Mark's death a few hours later, and he took it upon himself to do something for Mark's family, since they were now without their provider. A friend who worked for First Security Bank suggested setting up a memorial trust account on behalf of the family. Jack liked the idea, and they opened and established the Stall Memorial Trust Fund, into which funds could be deposited in any First Security branch throughout the city and state. This opportunity for sharing with the Stall family was then announced to the community through the media, and it sparked immediate response.

By the day of the funeral, several businesses throughout the Treasure Valley had already taken steps to have some part in helping the Stalls. The *Idaho Statesman* reported at least twenty-four businesses that indicated they were going to donate money or services to the family. Restaurants and businesses donated a percentage of their proceeds during certain periods, and garden nurseries set up money trees. Some area hotels donated rooms for out-of-town members of the family, while hair salons, hot-dog stands, and tire stores set aside a portion of their sales and services to aid the now-fatherless Stall family.

The Saturday night after the funeral, a candlelight vigil was scheduled at the shooting site in downtown Boise. Five hundred donated candles were distributed, and a Loomis Fargo and Company armored car was stationed at the site for donations.

The Boise Fire Department, along with the Boise Police Department, responded with significant financial sacrifices in order to help Mark's family. Three weeks after Mark's death, at a chili-feed and charity softball game between the Fire and Police departments on October 11 at Memorial Stadium in Boise, both departments had already raised or pledged nearly $30,000 for the family. Some of those monies would be provided on a monthly basis over the next year, to be drawn from future overtime earnings.

Cheryl was particularly touched by the sacrifices of the officers and firemen. She knew their general levels of pay, and therefore knew at what cost they were giving to her and her girls. She felt unworthy to be accepting such generous gifts, and easily wept over the sacrificial expressions of these caring people. She also knew that, were it an officer other than her husband, Mark himself would have felt as his brother-officer families now felt about helping his. Mark would have sacrificed without a second thought in order to help a family going through what his family now faced.

One day not long after the funeral, a Boise officer stopped by her home to say hello and check up on her, then handed her an envelope. He explained that he and his wife wanted to do something separate from other efforts in her behalf. They just wanted her to know she was special to them, and that she was in their hearts. When she opened the envelope and found three hundred dollars inside, she cried, for she knew that gift undoubtedly came at a sacrifice.

Schools and school children brought focus to this tragedy by participating in fundraising and by sending hundreds of handmade cards and messages to the family. And also, they gave—from a few dollars to hundreds of dollars. Some of the cards and messages were very touching. Teachers used this tragedy as a teaching tool for showing compassion and reinforcing respect for policemen and the law.

On October 16, 1997, less than a month after Mark's death, Cheryl agreed to speak briefly to sixth through eighth grade students at split assemblies at Meridian Middle School. Honored that day were the Meridian Police and Fire Departments. Governor Phil Batt gave a short talk, as did Meridian Mayor Bob Corrie.

When Cheryl stood to speak, she told the twelve hundred students and guests that they had choices to make and that they needed to be ready for the consequences of those choices. She also emphasized that they could make a lasting impression on someone, even at their young ages, and shared with them that they had collectively made an impression on her. Teachers later stated that these students had never been so quiet and respectful in an assembly. The school then presented Cheryl with a check for a thousand dollars, all raised by the student body.

Monies came to her from many different sources, including strangers from other states. One woman from Houston, Texas sent three hundred dollars. Gifts from police departments across the nation were sent. One especially meaningful gift came from a police department located near the Brodrick family in Pennsylvania. Their thoughtful gesture was especially appreciated for its moral significance.

In addition to gifts designated directly to Cheryl and her girls, there was also the opportunity for the community to contribute to the Idaho Peace Officers' Memorial Fund. This fund had been established a few years earlier by families and friends of officers who had died in the line of duty throughout Idaho.

The Peace Officers' Board of Directors had been raising funds to initiate and complete this project, but at the time of Mark's death the project was still languishing for lack of funds to build the memorial. Those involved with the project had been patiently striving to raise the needed monies, but successful completion of the memorial anytime soon did not seem to be very likely, the way things had been progressing. The interest of people and businesses in contributing to a death memorial project was not very high—until death struck home again on September 20, 1997.

By May 15, 1998, just under eight months after Mark's death, the beautiful Idaho memorial was completed and ready to be dedicated. It was dedicated that day on the date nationally designated as Law Enforcement Memorial Day, in a special, moving ceremony. The Memorial can be visited at the Idaho Department of Law Enforcement in Meridian, Idaho. The last name etched on the Memorial at the time of this writing was Mark Arlin Stall. Sadly, another name is already scheduled to be inscribed on the marble register—that of Trooper Linda Huff, the first woman in Idaho law enforcement history to be killed in the line of duty. Hers will be the fiftieth name.

The monies and responses given to Cheryl and her girls were overwhelming, but she often stated that she would far rather have her husband back and return to how it was before, struggles and all. The benefits and provisions coming to her because of the nature of Mark's death would obviously help her and the girls' futures, but all that support was a bitter trade for what they had lost. Having to face the future without their loved one could not be satisfactorily compensated, no matter how much money came to them.

Five months before his death Mark strongly felt that Cheryl and he should obtain some additional life insurance. Even the small amount they set aside for this would stretch them each month, but he felt compelled to do it. It was as though he sensed an urgency. They paid one hundred twenty-seven dollars in premiums on his part of the policy in those five months, an action that guaranteed his family a future. Of course, they didn't actually believe there would be an enacting of the policy provisions—they were much too young. Still, Mark felt it was necessary.

Money has been and always will be a poor substitute for establishing the value of a human life, yet it is the primary compensation for loss in this world. Cheryl would prefer, as would any widow like her, to have to scrape by financially and still have her husband than to live sumptuously without him. She had no choice, however—she no longer had a living husband. She had been left with a single, irreversible choice—to accept the gifts and kindnesses brought her way by Mark's mortality and try to forge ahead with what was left of her life. It was a terrible position to be in, and achingly empty.

The First Security Trust Fund for the Stall family reached almost ninety thousand dollars. It is being reported in this book so that the deep and sincere gratitude of Cheryl Stall and her daughters can be publicly expressed. The gifts have ranged from large to small, but all reflect the depth of compassion felt and expressed by hundreds and hundreds of people.

The loss to Cheryl Stall and her two young girls has been great. No amount of money, goods, or services can even remotely begin to compensate their deprivation. Nothing can replace the essence and vitality of Mark Stall as a human being and his presence with those he cherished. They loved him dearly and deeply grieve over his absence, but have no choice other than to go on living without him. However, the response to Mark's passing has been heartening—to Cheryl and her girls, and also to the rest of the family. Though their lives have been forever altered, and though they can never go back to what they were before, the path ahead is more manageable because of the compassion of multitudes of caring people.

To all, therefore, who have given to and shared with the Stall family, they express their deepest gratitude. You have helped immeasurably to make the way ahead a bit easier.

12

The Cross Controversy

On September 24, the day of Mark's funeral, an unexpected sequel to this tragedy began brewing. It would quickly turn ugly.

Two days earlier, a simple steel cross had been constructed and placed at the site of Mark's slaying. Thereafter, a steady flow of people began visiting the area surrounding the cross. While people had previously been driving by or stopping at the Rider's Bar parking lot, the visible cross attracted even more attention. It drew grieving people to the site out of curiosity, but it also provided the opportunity to place flowers, cards, and miscellaneous items in one central location. Street and foot traffic steadily grew at the site.

The placement of a cross to Mark's memory could not even be remotely foreseen as something that would stimulate controversy. It bore no name, nor was there a message of any kind attached to it. It was designed to be a simple marker at the spot where an honorable policeman died. The cross also, in this case, designated that Mark Stall had personally trusted in the cross of Christ to provide him forgiveness of sin.

However, that symbol took on a certain sacredness, and became revered for what it represented. Many people had been deeply touched by Mark's needless death and wanted to show their respect in some concrete way. Personal messages were left to him, as well as poems and praises for his sacrifice. Some people knelt there and prayed; many openly wept as they looked upon all the flowers and messages heaped around the gleaming white crosspieces. Some families even brought their children to the site and utilized this tragic situation to instruct them about the high cost of disrespecting proper authority. They would also learn, among many possible lessons, that sometimes the good guys lose.

Ultimately, Mark's cross and the effect it was having on the community stimulated some person or group of individuals to disparage Mark's death by erecting crosses to those who caused his death. Two wooden crosses, bearing the names of the Brodrick brothers, were placed in the ground less than twenty feet from where Mark's cross stood.

No one can know with certainty what went on in the minds of those who initiated this action, but it seemed then and still seems that these crosses were meant to be an "in your face" message to the Boise Police Department. It was a way of generating publicity that announced to the public at large that the "pigs" had again killed innocent people, but this time, in contrast to previous fatal shootings, one of their own also got it. Therefore, the crosses placed for the brothers were meant to denigrate the nobleness of Mark's death and to elevate, instead, the "innocent young men" his comrades killed. It is of interest that a former Boise resident who had moved to New England sent an e-mail warning that read, "Watch out for those who defend their cruel actions." That person had a sense from clear across the country of what might evolve in respect to support for the Brodricks.

Naive people believed that the placing of the crosses was meant to communicate one of several things: compassion for the Brodricks; an attempt to lessen the tensions between the police and the community; an expression of recognition that two other men had also died there; or that these foolish, misguided young men could be just as respected in death as the policeman. One elderly lady even brought beautiful memorial flowers to grace the Brodrick crosses, as though they were forgotten heroes who did not deserve to be ignored.

The actual intent of the other crosses was precisely the opposite. As already stated, they made a statement to both the police and the public: that the cops of Boise were trigger-happy and continued to mow down innocent people, and that the Brodricks had done nothing to warrant getting from the police what they did, and it was now time to recognize their innocence and their undeserved deaths by raising crosses in their memory. They further implied that the people of Boise and the Treasure Valley were being duped into standing behind their out-of-control, renegade cops.

By the time the Brodrick crosses first appeared on Wednesday, the day of Mark's funeral, the Boise Police Department had already received several threatening phone calls hinting violence against them. The Ada County Sheriff's office had also received an anonymous letter that threatened police agencies in general. The potential for violence against the police represented by these kinds of behaviors was not taken lightly. The possibility of angry, vengeful individuals taking some kind of action was taken so seriously that, as a safety precaution, the Boise State University Pavilion underwent a bomb sweep the morning of the funeral. While these kinds of procedures are standard for large gatherings, for this particular event—a police funeral—the possibility for trouble was even more heightened.

Arnold Rubey personally received one anonymous phone call suggesting that his son-in-law's comrades were not innocent in the Brodrick shooting; that Mark and his friends were actually the aggressors in this shooting and that eventually this would be verified as truth. The caller told Arnold he just wanted to do him a favor by making sure he didn't close his mind to the truth, and urged that he not accept what he was told just because his son-in-law was a cop, albeit a dead one.

On another occasion Arnold was at the site of the shooting when a curious-acting man strode into the Rider's parking lot and began measuring and pacing out the scene. He didn't even look over the area, just intently started doing his thing. He was animated and huffy in his movements, as though disgusted about something. He seemed to want the people around to understand that he was there to discover the real truth about the shooting—whatever truth could be ascertained according to a tape measure. When people asked who he was, no one knew, not even the police.

Even paramedics experienced a certain amount of animosity during this time. A few days after Mark's shooting, one unit stopped at the Albertson's food store on State Street to pick up something to eat. Just as they parked some men in a car in front of them shouted expletives at them about the blue ribbon on their antenna that showed support for the police. One of them then made a gun motion at them with a pointed finger. The paramedics drove off without going into the store. The anti-police attitude of these men was taken seriously, since a gunshot had been fired at or near their unit while they were en route to a call during that time. One paramedic clearly heard the shot, and the other saw the barrel flash.

The two crosses did not last—they were broken into pieces and thrown into the street before the day was over. As would be expected, the public took offense over the fact that someone actually had the audacity to erect crosses to honor men who had killed one of their policemen. *At least do it somewhere else if you choose to do it,* was the thought. But then, since the intention of this act was to stir up contention, this was the place that would maximize the conflict. To put up crosses somewhere else would attract little or no attention.

Other crosses soon appeared. One woman, who frequently visited the scene because of the emotion she felt over Mark's death, became so incensed that she personally participated in tearing down two sets of crosses. Another woman brought horse manure and dumped it on the area around the Brodrick crosses. Someone else erected a sign designating the area around the brothers' crosses as a "spitting area."

Back and forth it went. Crosses would be re-erected, and down they would go. At one point there were three crosses in the Brodrick area—two to represent the Brodricks, and a third to apparently represent Christ dying on the cross for them.

Those at the center of the cross controversy were generating publicity, column space, and airtime that were causing serious tensions to build, and the possibility of an ugly confrontation continued to escalate. The last thing the Stall family wanted or needed was for someone to get hurt or killed over this nonsense. A candlelight vigil was scheduled on Saturday night at Mark's cross, and if the additional crosses remained at the center of growing tensions, something unpleasant was likely to happen there. It was unlikely that the "in your face" crowd would back off. One young man, who seemed to be the primary force in the first crosses erected to the Brodricks, said he would continue to erect crosses until the officer's cross was removed. In other words, the officer's cross did not deserve to be there.

The Stall family was not immediately aware of the controversy. Because they were still coping with fresh grief, they were not exposing themselves to media coverage. However, when they found out that crosses had been erected to the Brodricks at the shooting site, they were stunned at the crass insensitivity of such an act. Eventually, though they had nothing to do with the creation of this controversy, they felt they might have to do something to help diffuse tensions.

They discussed what they could do and decided to issue some kind of statement regarding the cross controversy, which would inform the community of their concerns. They also decided that Friday night during the ten o'clock news hour might give the most exposure, as all the local channels would get the statement out simultaneously. The police station on Barrister Drive was selected as the safest place to do this.

After coming to this decision, they ran into difficulty reaching a consensus about what they could or should do and what they should include in the statement. They had no right to remove the Brodrick crosses, of course, nor did they desire to get embroiled in conflict with those who were placing them. Though the Brodrick crosses were distasteful to them, their pain over Mark's death was burden enough to bear. But if something tragic happened to a citizen or to an officer because of the conflict over the crosses, it would add further to their sorrow.

Back and forth they went. They were aware that Chief Paulson was concerned about where this situation might go, as were officers who had been observing the escalating tensions over the previous three days. This was tailor-made stuff for those who wanted to suck the police into more controversy. The one area in which the Stall family had freedom to take action pertained to the removal of Mark's cross. All were reluctant to remove the cross, but some felt that was what they were going to have to do. Cheryl did not want to at all. Most of all, and rightly so, she felt that Mark deserved to have that cross there because it was there he had sacrificed his life while doing his duty. There was no argument on that point. She also felt it would appear that the negative elements in the community had won the battle. Most importantly, she believed it would offend the officers who were there with Mark facing the same danger, and that it would disappoint the entire police department.

Her points were viable; everyone emotionally and rationally agreed with them. No one wanted to remove the cross, and it seemed ludicrous to even have to consider such a matter. But they were forced to deal with a volatile situation that they alone might have the best chance to diffuse. They could not leave the problem in the hands of the police, because those wanting the controversy in the first place weren't going allow the situation to quiet down–this turmoil and attention were precisely what they wanted. Boise's police department could not afford to have another situation on their hands.

Finally the family agreed that, at this point, they would not remove Mark's cross, and that they would make an appeal to the community to avoid adding to the upset over the crosses. They scrambled to prepare their statement, and then Ray and Arnold rushed to the police station just barely in time to get it on the air during the ten o'clock news. The statement read as follows:

> On behalf of the families of Officer Mark Stall, we would like to publicly thank the city of Boise for your overwhelming expression of love and support in our time of loss.
>
> We are disheartened by the controversy that now surrounds the site of last Saturday morning's incident. The cross located at the site was placed there to symbolize that Mark honored and followed Jesus Christ to the point that he gave his life fulfilling the career God called him to.
>
> In light of this, we are asking the public to please conduct yourselves in a manner that would best facilitate the peace Mark gave his life to uphold.
>
> For those desirous of further honoring Mark, we respectfully ask that you honor his memory by spending time with your families and worshiping at a local church.
>
> In closing, it is our desire that you would pray for each of the families involved in this tragic situation. Thank you. Thank you very much.

The statement did little to settle anything down, other than make it hard on those who wished to defend Mark's honor by resisting the tributes to the brothers. Brodrick supporters continued to show up at the scene and exchange barbs with those who took exception to their tasteless actions. Tensions continued to mount. The police were so concerned about the weekend nights that they posted personnel all around the site in case more serious problems arose. The whole thing had escalated to an absurd degree.

The *Idaho Press-Tribune* reported in their Saturday edition that the slain officer's family was upset with the vandalism at the site of the shoot-out. They completely missed the point. Vandalism was not the issue—the vandalism part of the situation was petty—the controversy itself was their concern. The real problem lay in the reason the Brodrick crosses were erected in the first place, which was to convey an attitude of disrespect and resistance to honoring the death of a policeman by a cross placed there in his memory. In a sense, the additional crosses were incidental—the real intent was to stir things up. The family was not ignorant as to why this was happening, but it was troubling and disappointing nonetheless.

The family was unified in its opinion that the crosses placed in honor of the Brodricks were totally inappropriate because of the brothers' brutal and callous murder of their loved one, Mark Stall. It was repulsive to them to think that this kind of honor would even be considered for people who maliciously snuffed out a good man's life. The Brodrick brothers have souls, like everyone else, and will answer to God, like everyone else; but such a gesture was beyond the scope of dignity. The cross controversy should have never happened—it was beyond tasteless.

By Saturday afternoon, Cheryl reluctantly agreed that it would be best to remove the cross—things were getting too dangerous. It was hugely repulsive to her to do this, as it was to all the family, but it now seemed they had little choice if they wanted this vulgar controversy to stop. They therefore arranged for several men to be at the candlelight vigil Saturday night with shovels and a pickup, so that when the time was appropriate, the cross could be dug up and quickly removed.

Several family members attended the vigil on Saturday night, including Cheryl. A large crowd had gathered, and the Loomis Fargo and Company armored truck was on scene. All the networks had teams covering the event, but none knew what was coming in respect to the cross.

When darkness was fully over the city and the main part of the vigil was over, Cheryl quietly slipped out of the crowd so she would not see the cross removal. When she was gone, Arnold announced to those present that Mark's cross was going to be removed. He stated that Mark's death site was not intended to be a shrine or a sacred location, but simply a place where a man laid down his life. As a family working through the emotions and changes revolving around Mark's death, they just wanted to move forward and learn to live with their loss.

The crowd was stunned, as were the news reporters. They had all been caught off guard.

The men immediately began digging. The cross was encased in concrete, which made their task slower, but they soon had it wedged loose. They had to take the cross with the concrete still cemented on the end. It was quickly loaded into a pickup and taken away. Mark's cross, earned at terrible cost and displayed for six days, was gone. A few weeks later that cross would be erected on Mark's grave at Dry Creek Cemetery as his memorial until his permanent headstone was ready.

Shortly afterwards, even in the presence of overwhelmingly sympathetic response for Mark Stall and the Boise Police Department, two more crosses to the Brodricks were erected. With or without the cop's cross, these people were determined to continue to honor the Brodricks and stick it in the face of the community and the police—the intent was very clear by this time. Within two days, however, even the Brodrick crosses disappeared for good. No one was paying attention to them by that time, so there was no reason to continue their placement.

There was one other disappointing reaction and response regarding the crosses, when a Boise city council member spoke a few days later about being shocked and appalled at the desecration of the crosses for the two brothers. This particular reaction from a city official was appalling in itself. Was the scattering of those sticks of wood the biggest issue to comment on in this tragedy, especially when it was an act of defiance to place those crosses in the first place? Was there actually more concern over defending the posthumous rights of the violent Brodrick brothers than there was to staunchly decry their evil act of murdering Mark Stall? Was there not enough repulsion over the senseless killing of Mark Stall as to denounce that despicable act, and then have the courage instead to go on record as defending the police force and the sacrifices they made for their city? It was hugely disappointing to observe the political jockeying that took place as officials took care to not offend those who openly bashed the police at every possible opportunity.

That there are those who have an agenda to trash the police and defend evildoers is evident. They speak to a certain audience, and are furthered along by being provided column-space, airtime, and other platforms whereby they can inform the public about how bad their police are. Their perspective has one prevailing premise: the police are almost always wrong, and those confronted by those same police are almost always innocent. As a result of this perspective, their goal for the public to embrace is two-fold: one, to elevate and excuse rebels; and two, to reduce confidence in law enforcement. Sadly, many of our leaders, both locally and nationally, give credence to this backwards kind of thinking. This then leaves the police wondering about how worthwhile it is to confront wrongdoing and put themselves at risk, when they may be the ones on the hot seat instead of those involved in the wrongdoing.

One Boise citizen commented about what he viewed as the lack of balance in the outpouring and outcry over the young people who had died at the hands of the Boise police in previous months, and the officer who was killed. The answer to that should be rather obvious—the officer was a duly sworn peace officer who was doing his job, as were the officers in the other referred-to incidents. Furthermore, the young men were each and every one acting in defiance and physical resistance to the police. What is there to balance? Why should there be an outpouring of support for defiant, rebellious behavior? This is precisely why the Brodrick crosses were inappropriate: the brothers were murderers. How did we come to this twisted point where evil is honored and good is trashed?

Shortly after Mark's funeral, another person reflected similar thinking in a letter to the editor at the *Idaho Statesman*. He wrote: "Hey, Boise, nice cop parade. Now do we have one for the two brothers riddled with thirty-two holes? What about the kid recently shot in the head? Or that drunk downtown last spring? How about a funeral procession for all traffic violators?

"Boise, now is not the time to rally around the Boise Police 'excessive' force, but to investigate the over-hyped budget and under-trained tactics that guide our pallbearers in blue."

This individual is representative of a certain mindset that hates cops and cherishes troublemakers. These people exercise a twisted logic in which perpetrators of crimes or violence are not held responsible for what they do, but those who confront them are the bad people. The frightening part about such attitudes is that these individuals and others like them are likely to be among those who draw the police to them with their anti-authority belligerence or law-breaking behaviors. They dwell on the edge of the law, and therefore stir up trouble, knowing the police will be somewhere around because of it. When the police are in fact around, and when they confront the trouble they've been hired to deal with, they often end up being the ones put on trial in the arena of public opinion for being mean-spirited and abusive to the perpetrators.

Somewhere, somehow, in this and every other community, the buck has to stop where it belongs—with the evildoer, who will be held responsible for his or her behavior as well as for the subsequent consequences of that behavior. Blame-shifting everything onto the police each time lawlessness is dealt with has gotten old. It would be refreshing to hear of someone who has done wrong taking responsibility for it instead of always making the police the culprits.

The Boise cross controversy, in a rather morbid way, brought this anti-cop attitude to the surface. It became an eye-opener as to the level of tolerance for evil behavior that we now allow in our society. When good and honorable policemen are made the villains in deadly situations, we have crossed the line of decency that is necessary for an ordered and respectful society. We cannot forsake the higher standard of right in order to excuse wrongdoing.

A final word. After Idaho Trooper Linda Huff was shot to death in June 1998, there were several complaints in letters to the editor and on radio talk shows. Some citizens bemoaned the expense to taxpayers of police funerals, the inconvenience to the public of having highways closed for a period of time, and the high ceremony in honoring the deaths of those in law enforcement.

These people fail to consider that the families of these slain officers have been deprived and inconvenienced for a lifetime. Evil people ruthlessly killed their loved ones because of what they represented as peace officers, and now their families can't have them back. They lost their lives because of their job, their uniform, and their badge.

Also, the police are hired and legally commissioned by cities, counties, and states to provide protection and law enforcement in behalf of their citizens. They are required to carry guns and to have available other protective gear like ballistic vests, because of the kind of people with whom they have to deal. They constitute a unique vocation, a brotherhood, a family of mutual protectors who often have to assist their fellow officers with unruly situations.

In any case, be it Mark Stall, Linda Huff, or any of the dozens of other officers every year in America who are sacrificed to death by heartless thugs just because they were doing their duty—it is demoralizing to hear such complaints and to see their heartbroken families subjected to such insensitive and heartless reasoning. The dollars spent and the brief inconveniences are a small price indeed compared to the life-long losses suffered by law enforcement families who lose a loved one in the line of duty. Allow them this public honor for serving you, the public, at such sacrifice.

A simple white cross is not enough.

13

Big Guns Aimed at Boise

On the night of June 17, 1998, Trooper Linda Huff was murdered in Coeur d'Alene, Idaho in the parking lot of the Idaho State Police department. After her June 23 funeral at the Idaho Center in Nampa, Idaho, anti-police graffiti appeared at the C. Ben Ross Reservoir south of the small Idaho community of Indian Hills. The writings did not mention Linda Huff directly, but they distinctly demeaned Idaho law enforcement. They also mentioned the Brodrick brothers, who had now been dead nine months. It is curious that these messages appeared when they did.

Among the inscriptions were "Police State" and "Brodrick brothers our heroes. They died for them. Would you?" These words were sprayed on garbage cans and outhouses. Obviously the brothers' deaths remained a significant issue with some people, who consider them to be martyrs and true heroes.

While it remains unclear what was meant by "They died for them," the other phrases are easily deciphered: the police are the real problem in this state because of their authoritarian attitudes, and the true heroes are individuals like the Brodricks, who died for the cause (whatever that cause may be). Are there others of you who will stand up and do the same?

The nature of these expressions suggests that there is a brotherhood of those with anti-authoritarian attitudes. It is implied that the Brodricks subscribed to such a philosophy and that numerous others are like them in spirit. The graffiti at the reservoir was a cheap way to state that position.

Area families took up a collection to clean up the graffiti. Before they removed the writings, though, some of them took their children to the site to show them what the unsavory side of hate can result in.

The Brodricks certainly have not been forgotten. Their deaths continue to be raised as an example that the Boise police and law enforcement throughout Idaho are aggressive and destructive powermongers wishing to harm people and ignore civil rights. This attitude transcends Boise, for it exists in many communities, reflective of a resistive, anti-authoritarian movement that increasingly boasts advocates throughout the nation. Not all who resist authority do so with wicked intentions, but some are geared to doing their evil in such a manner that the police end up being scorned for hindering the freedom of the wrongdoer to do evil things.

Without a doubt the Brodrick shooting caused a sensation, not only in the Treasure Valley and the state of Idaho, but across the country. Even very large cities more accustomed to shootings and greater amounts of day-to-day crime than Boise, took notice of this particular gun battle. Most people were shocked to hear that sixty-two rounds of ammunition were fired, fifty-two by the police and ten by the Brodricks. Craig Brodrick suffered twenty-six wounds, and his brother Doug sustained seven.

As a result, a cry immediately went up protesting the brutality of the Boise police in senselessly pumping too many bullets into these two men. How many bullets does it take to kill a person? In the case of Mark Stall it took one; in the case of Craig Brodrick, it took many, until he was finally stopped from continuing to fire.

It was natural that the family of Craig and Doug Brodrick would be stunned and broken to hear of the deaths of their sons, especially when their deaths were so violent. Their desire to know how and why their sons died was certainly well justified. Their deaths occurred twenty-five hundred miles away, in a distant state and city where several other young men had been killed at the hands of that city's police force in the past year and a half. The mind wants straight answers, since the number of bullets in this shooting was almost beyond belief. No one could fault Martin and Patricia Brodrick for wanting to understand what had happened.

Because of the distance of Idaho from Pennsylvania, and since they were apparently dubious about expecting truth to come out of the region where this happened, they hired a well-known forensic pathologist, Cyril Wecht of Pittsburgh, to conduct another autopsy on their sons' bodies when they arrived in Pennsylvania. Wecht is the coroner in Allegheny County, which includes Pittsburgh, and is a well-known witness pathologist. He has studied the autopsies of the very famous—people such as President John F. Kennedy, Robert Kennedy, Elvis Presley, and others. His 1993 book, *Cause of Death,* presents his conclusions on a number of high-profile cases.

On Thursday, September 25, the day after Mark's Boise funeral and the day before the Brodrick funerals in Homer City, Pennsylvania, Wecht conducted a news conference following his examination of the two brothers. He concluded that they were "shot too many times" (one assumes he means overkill). He also emphasized that the fact that some shots were fired at relatively close range would add significance to this case. He did not elaborate on what that significance might be.

He further stated that in his thirty-five years of forensic work, excluding some gangland slayings, he could not remember a case in which two people were as riddled with bullets as these two men were.

He then made some rather bizarre statements about the state of Idaho. He labeled the state as "different," saying that there exists in Idaho a militia mentality, and that there is a different attitude held by both police and citizens. Then he threw in the name of Mark Fuhrman as being from Idaho, as though that confirmed the baseness of the state. Fuhrman, the retired LAPD detective who became a significant figure in the O.J. Simpson murder trial, purchased property in northern Idaho several years ago and now has a home there. Wecht seemed to suggest that Mark Fuhrman did not move to Idaho "because it happened to be next to California," but because of the prevalent militia mentality. This mention of Fuhrman was apparently meant to add to Wecht's notion that bad cops are all over Idaho.

Wecht admitted that his opinion of the state was based on news accounts of Idaho events, particularly the well-known Ruby Ridge incident in 1992. Ironically, it strikes many Idahoans that the militia mentality Wecht alluded to was certainly evident in the two young men from his state of Pennsylvania who used their guns to kill another human being on September 20, 1997. Based on his line of reasoning, their act makes Pennsylvania a bad state.

Dr. Wecht also stated that the Brodricks were not speeding or fleeing the police and that there was no apparent reason for shooting to have commenced. That assessment is accurate, and most people who have some familiarity with the case are baffled as to why the brothers made a decision to shoot it out. Wecht made no attempt to explain why Craig Brodrick evidently wanted to bait the police to stop them, for both he and his brother knew full well that a police car was following them. An Idaho Power Company security camera, taping the street at Twelfth and Idaho that night, showed a vehicle changing lanes and a police car close behind at the time of this incident. The car was the one driven by Craig Brodrick. On at least two occasions, according to the reports of the officers involved, Craig abruptly changed lanes without signaling while the police were on their tail. To deliberately make such moves without attempting to signal is a sure invitation to being stopped by those same police.

Ada County Coroner Erwin Sonnenberg, who performed the autopsies on the brothers as well as on Mark Stall, expressed concerns about Wecht's public comments. Sonnenberg, who is president of the International Association of Coroners and Medical Examiners, stated that he found it "...very unusual that he (Wecht) would be making a lot of statements without looking at the evidence we have here. I would expect him to come out here and look at what we've got."

It would be a long while before Sonnenberg's office received a request from anyone, particularly Dr. Wecht, requesting records of the forensic work his office had conducted in this case. Eventually those findings and autopsy records were, at Dr. Wecht's request, provided to his office.

A couple of weeks later, in early October 1997, the Brodrick family took another major step by bringing famed criminal lawyer F. Lee Bailey into the case. He was asked to represent them in looking into the possible filing of a civil rights lawsuit. Cyril Wecht and F. Lee Bailey have been close friends for many years, according to the foreword written by Bailey in Wecht's *Cause of Death*, which would explain how Bailey was brought into this case.

Once again at a Pittsburgh news conference, with Bailey doing the talking this time, statements filled with insinuations about what really happened in Boise were freely tossed out.

Bailey questioned whether the police had actually fired in self-defense against the Brodricks, and even suggested that Mark Stall may have been killed by a bullet from another policeman.

He further stated that the thought of two brothers "taking on seven police officers in bulletproof vests is insane, and I'm betting it didn't happen." He added that he would press the FBI to conduct an investigation, but if nothing came of that, he would file a lawsuit claiming the civil rights of the brothers were violated. This move on Bailey's part—the request for an FBI investigation—tends to leave an impression that there is something definitely wrong with the police version of the events; that the FBI itself has suspicions about what the police have reported. This simply is not the case. When the FBI does get involved, which is quite often in cases of this nature around the country, they do a complete review of all aspects of the case, then report the facts according to their findings.

Apparently F. Lee Bailey had not listened to Bryan Hagler's tape recording of the shooting, which had been broadcast all across the country less than twenty-four hours after the shooting. That tape clearly reveals that the presence of seven officers did not deter either Craig or Doug Brodrick from pulling weapons and taking them on.

Furthermore, Bailey had not yet done enough homework to know that Mark Stall had been shot by a forty-caliber bullet which matched the weapon of Doug Brodrick. With this information already available, it was totally misleading and inaccurate to suggest that Mark may have been shot by one of his own team members. An even wilder suggestion emerged sometime later in Boise: Mark Stall was such a straight cop that he was about to rat on the Boise Police Department about their past transgressions, and so was eliminated by his own team members to cover up their dirty deeds! The purpose of any of these preposterous ideas is to make people question what they have been told by the police and begin being receptive to different possibilities, even far-fetched ones. The door of doubt is cracked open, in order that a foundation may be laid for the later crafting of a scenario that may best form the basis for a lawsuit.

Martin Brodrick, father of Craig and Doug, stated that his sons were too smart to fight with the police; that they had in fact desired to become Pennsylvania state troopers and had made application for such positions.

Whether they were too smart to fight with police is obviously questionable in light of what actually took place and as verified by the tape recording of the incident. Also, Craig reportedly carried a gun quite often. He was described by co-workers and other acquaintances as racist, anti-government, and pro-Hitler. In July 1997, a couple of months after Craig had moved to Boise, a friend called on him at his apartment. She reported seeing only a card table, folding chairs, and several long, narrow boxes leaning against the living room walls. She did not know what was in the boxes, but she did see rounds of ammunition stacked on the kitchen counter.

Doug Brodrick, the younger of the two, was said to glorify conflict and to freely talk about killing in a joking manner. He was described as liking outlaw country music, which tended to match his militia-like philosophy on life. His attitude was said by one individual to reflect a perspective of "kill them all and let God sort them out."

He reportedly talked often about death, and told at least one person that he had no problem with killing someone. He commented to one woman that, "I'm mean, meaner than hell," then went on to tell her that he felt like he was going to kill somebody.

One co-worker remembers Doug saying that if he were ever pulled over in a confrontation with the cops, he would shoot the cop. Another co-worker stated that on one occasion he and Doug Brodrick saw someone pulled over by the Boise Police where they worked, then discussed how one might try to get out of the ticket. Doug's response: "Shoot the cop!"

Craig once talked to a co-worker about the subject of blowing up a federal building, then went on to say that Doug was crazier than he was.

Were the brothers too smart to take on the police? It doesn't appear so. A supervisor where the brothers worked stated that on Friday, September 19, the day preceding that night's shooting, Craig's behavior was different than usual that afternoon and evening at work. It was evident that he was down. Around midnight, an hour or so after he and Doug had left work, he was apparently still uptight over whatever had been troubling him throughout that day. He and Doug evidently made a stop at the Torch Lounge, where they had confrontations with patrons in the bar, and Doug made it plain that it would be inadvisable to mess with his brother because he was ready to go ballistic on somebody. Both were eventually tossed out of the Torch because one was seen to have a gun.

To say that Craig and Doug were not looking for trouble is equally disputable from another viewpoint. To begin with, each of them had a semi-automatic pistol, and when Craig's clothing and body were examined after the shooting, several additional weapons were found on his person. He had a holster on his left waist, which had held the gun he used to fire at the officers; a knife was tucked into a sheath on the right side of his waist with the holster and sheath held by a police belt; an knife with an eight-inch blade was attached to the ankle area of his left leg; and a seven-and-a-half inch plastic throwing knife was attached to the ankle area of his right leg. He had four weapons on him when he stepped out of the car for the last time in the Rider's lot. Also found hidden, in a slit in the back of his belt, was a handcuff key. Was he expecting he might be hand-cuffed sometime and would need a way to free his hands?

The number of bullets that went into or through the brothers is easily explained. Six of the seven officers at the scene ended up firing at the two with semi-automatic weapons—only one officer did not have his weapon out before or during the shooting. Incredibly, Craig Brodrick took several bullets while still managing to move around the front of the car to the passenger side before he went down to stay. As he was moving and firing his own weapon, he continued to be fired upon. It was remarkable that he could take so many bullets yet continue to still be in motion.

The rush of adrenaline, surge of emotions, and delayed physical responses to being gravely wounded can sometimes keep a person going for several seconds—as long as fifteen seconds, according to medical people—before the physiological processes caused by serious body wounds are fully enacted. Craig Brodrick's ability to keep going with so much lead entering his body was nothing short of amazing. Mark Stall, mortally wounded from one bullet, was still able to fire his gun at least once more after being hit, and after he fell to the ground. He was probably paralyzed from his wound, but the shut-down of the body from bullet damage was delayed for a few seconds.

Cyril Wecht and F. Lee Bailey had questions, which is a reasonable thing to expect. Many other people also had questions, and still do, because of the severity of the gun-battle and the controversies that arose afterwards.

The Stall family also has questions. Why would two young men foolishly and callously choose to challenge seven officers in an open gun battle, knowing that such actions would surely result in their own deaths? Had they in the past decided to take on a cop or cops with the intention to kill? Did they live with some kind of morbid death wish to do their thing when the time was right and go down in a blaze of glory? If so, did they impulsively agree together under the circumstances that evolved on September 20, 1997 to try to kill whatever cops they could, though they would likely go down themselves? What could they possibly have been thinking about that was even close to rational?

F. Lee Bailey, or someone else, for that matter, may file a civil lawsuit in behalf of the Brodrick family. No matter what is forthcoming in that regard, it seems ethically vulgar to sue the city of Boise and the Boise Police Department for violating the civil rights of two men who, of their own volition, needlessly chose to fire their weapons at the police. In so doing, they killed one policeman and seriously wounded another. Do you then sue the people who in fear defended their own lives when fired upon? Do you sue their city's police department and the rest of the city for having these officers on the streets to protect their citizens and to enforce their laws? Or have we come to a point where the police are expected to be mind readers, and even then, wait without reacting to forthcoming acts of violence? If so, they would already be well on the way to their own deaths, if they were expected to be non-reactive until a gun is first actually fired at them. This illogical perspective flies in the face of reason.

If anything, the assignment of blame leads directly back to the Brodrick brothers. They violated the civil rights of every human being they fired at that morning. Every officer there was traumatized by what he experienced in those awful seconds. Ron Winegar's civil rights were directly violated by the wounds unnecessarily inflicted upon him, along with the pain and physical restrictions he will now deal with for the rest of his life. The ride-along passengers were also subjected to the perverse violence initiated by the brothers. They will never forget the horror of what they saw and experienced that morning.

And last of all...what about Mark Stall's civil rights? His life is irretrievably gone. His family has been deprived of his presence forever. His civil rights were the most violated of all. What price do we assign to the worth of his life?

14

Life Can Never Be the Same

On a Saturday following the May 1998 dedication of the Idaho Peace Officers' Memorial in Meridian, Idaho, Arnold met Jodi Pogue-Turner at the Memorial. Jodi's father, William Pogue, and co-officer Wilson Elms were brutally murdered in 1981 while serving as officers for the Idaho Department of Fish and Game. Elms's body was thrown into the river by his murderer, and Pogue's body was taken elsewhere and buried in a shallow grave. When the few remains of Pogue's body were found, over twenty months later, there was little left to bury or cremate. It was an experience of the worst kind for the family.

Jodi, who served on the Peace Officers' Memorial Committee, shared with Arnold how much this memorial meant to her as the daughter of a man who had lost his life doing his duty. It gave her an additional amount of closure to the tragedy that had so deeply touched her family. It provided a unique place to mourn her father, since his ashes had been scattered in the Sawtooth Mountains of Idaho. Though seventeen years had passed, the pain and loss of her father's violent death remained vivid. The intensity of the loss has subsided over the years, but the trauma associated with his death remains an awful memory that cannot be erased. The Memorial, therefore, will always be a special place for survivor families like hers to remember and be remembered.

Jodi's sister, Linda Pogue-Rupe, wrote Cheryl a letter two days after Mark's death. She said, "Upon hearing the news Saturday morning of Mark's death, my heart sank to my feet, bringing back painful memories of my own. I will never forget how I felt sixteen years ago when I was told that my father had been killed while trying to arrest a poacher. Over the course of the week that followed, my mother, my sisters, my brother, and I huddled together, frightened, trying to sort out what had just shattered our lives."

Now, a new widow and her daughters faced a similar experience of pain and loss—one that will remain with them for their lifetimes. They were instantly thrust into a kind of grief that few people really understand—not that other young men do not die, but because of the nature of their loss since it was caused by a violent murder. Yet, they have no choice—they have been forced to drink from this cup of bitterness each and every new day they face. Even as they make the effort to focus on other things and to participate in activities of a happier nature, the voice of reality is never silent: Mark is dead; he is gone; things are different; nothing is the same anymore.

Friends and strangers alike wondered how Cheryl would cope in both the short and long haul; and how the two young girls would fare as the weeks, months, then years of living with such a loss unfolded.

Cheryl found herself uniquely alone, though surrounded by parents, family, and friends. She was now solely responsible for the wellbeing of her family, while being overwhelmed with her own grief at the same time. The yearning to run somewhere, anywhere, to escape the pain beckoned her, yet she knew she could not leave the pain behind no matter where she went. Likewise, the girls could not avoid the reality that their daddy was gone and would never be back again. They have no possibility of forgetting, for they, too, are daughters of a slain officer.

The Stall family was now in process of being reshaped, forced to adjust to unfamiliar and undesired circumstances. The old and familiar realities had suddenly ceased to be, and everything pertaining to their lives felt new and different. It was hard to let go of the old order as it existed when Mark was alive, but it had to be done. Underneath everything was the constant subconscious longing to have Mark back and for this to never have happened; but then the raw awareness of his absence would again shock them back to reality. The shadows of memory, the images of past events, and varied

September 2, 1989—Mark Stall and Cheryl Rubey are united in marriage in Sun Valley, California.

December 1994—Mark Arlin Stall is sworn in as a City of Boise police officer. His hire number was 512.

This message at Mark and Cheryl's church reflected their loss, but also their confidence in Mark's destiny.

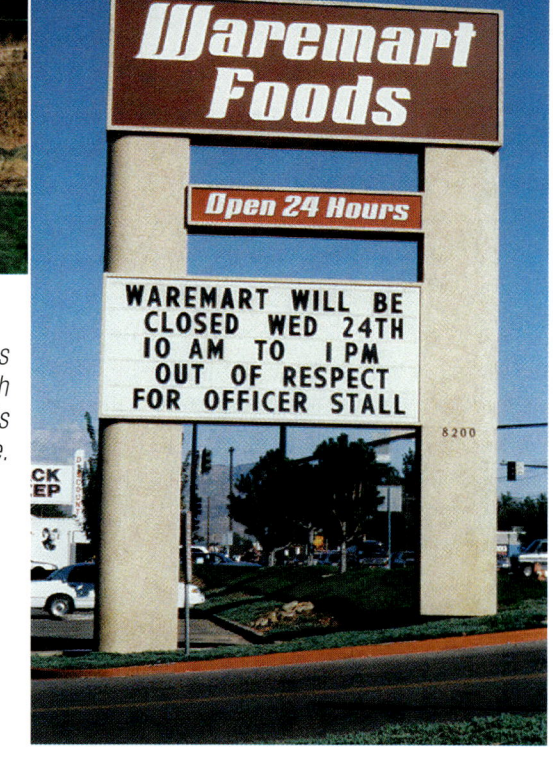

One of dozens of signs throughout Boise which honored Mark and his sacrifice.

The Boise Police Department retired Mark's locker and sealed it with momentos.

Mounds of flowers, cards, and flags from a grieving community drape a cross at the site of Mark's slaying.

September 24, 1997—the procession is about to begin from Cheryl's home.

Mark's flag-draped casket rests in place during the funeral service at the Boise State Pavilion. Officer John Terry eulogizes his friend, after which he presented Mark with his own Medal of Honor.

A panoramic view of the massive crowd at Dry Creek Cemetery following the earlier service at the Pavilion.

Some of the Stall family at Mark's gravesite the day after the funeral. The shock of their loss is evident.

FOR MARK STALL, THE BEST DADDY IN THE WHOLE WORLD!
LOVE - CHERYL, JONELLE, AND JULIA

The freshly installed memorial bench that overlooks Mark's gravesite.

Jonelle and Julia Stall placing bricks at the Idaho Peace Officers Memorial in Meridian, Idaho. The Memorial was dedicated on May 15, 1998

Jonelle and Julia Stall at the National Law Enforcement Officers Memorial in Washington D.C. Julia holds a candle from the candlelight vigil, and Jonelle's hand rests below Mark's name.

Larry Paulson, Boise Police Chief, is flanked by three newly sworn officers in his department: Mark Stall, Mark Vucinich, and Ron Alexx. It was December 1994.

Cheryl, Jonelle and Julia Stall with Gregory Casey, Sergeant At Arms of the U.S. Senate in May 1998. Greg lost two officers in his U.S. Capitol Police force two months later in a shooting within the U.S. Capitol.

Twenty-five members of the Stall-Rubey families in Washington D.C. with U.S. Senator (now Idaho Governor) Dirk Kempthorne. Officer Rob Berrier and wife Amy accompanied them for National Police Week in May 1998.

November 17, 1998, Cheryl and both girls send messages tied to balloons into the heavens. This would have been Mark's 31st birthday.

At the crest of the hill above Mark's final resting-place. The riderless horse strikes the "End of the Trail" pose.

The last photo taken of Mark Stall and his two girls on his and Cheryl's 8th anniversary, September 2, 1997. The shadows and his pensive mood reflect the darkness brought on by his death less than three weeks later.

The six daughters of Courtney and Cheryl Stall-Chamberlain on their wedding day, June 27, 1998.

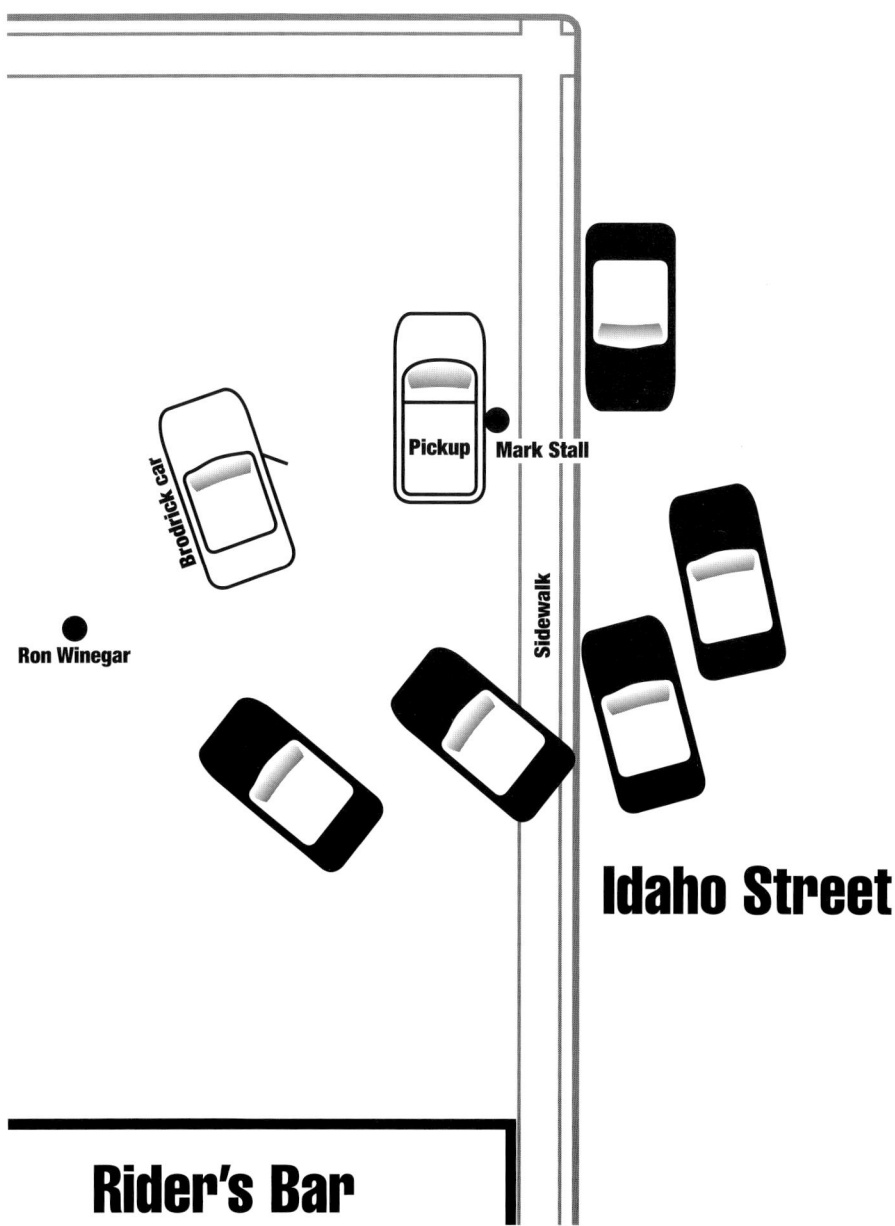

15th Street

Brodrick car

Pickup

Mark Stall

Ron Winegar

Sidewalk

Idaho Street

Rider's Bar

Diagram of the shooting scene adapted from detective Dave Smith's records. The location of officers Ron Winegar and Mark stall at the time of the shooting are noted.

The Mark Stall family as seen by the community. This picture was repeatedly printed and telecast in 1997.

recollections were all that were left. The person who once was such a part of the normal flow of their lives was forever gone from earth.

A heart-wrenching example of how change had touched their lives occurred during a visit to Mark's grave three or four weeks after his death. Cheryl, the girls, and the Rubeys stopped at the cemetery office to tend to details related to Mark's burial, and afterwards they went to the grave. Every visit there in those first weeks was extremely emotional, and this visit was no different. After a few sober moments staring at the fresh outline of the burial and the flowers left by visitors, Cheryl and her mother walked to an adjoining section of the cemetery to look at headstones for ideas for Mark's future stone. Arnold and the girls lingered behind.

When they were ready to leave, Julia said, "Papa, I want to hold you." He picked her up and held her close, sensing the terrible sadness that these two girls felt. Jonelle put her hand in his, and they turned to leave. They had walked only a few feet when Julia, looking back on her daddy's grave, loudly called out, "Bye-bye, Daddy. I love you." Jonelle also stopped, turned back, and called out to him. Arnold was so overcome by these tender expressions of love to their father that he instantly welled up with tears. The meaning in these good-byes from the heartbroken girls and the vacuum they felt from being without him were almost too much to bear.

A month after Mark's death, the family and the Boise police department were buoyed up by a two-day visit from Robert Vernon, retired Assistant Chief of the Los Angeles Police Department. Bob had had a "timely" cancellation in his very busy schedule of travel and speaking around the world, and graciously agreed to come to Boise to spend time with the police department and meet with the family.

The Rubeys already knew Bob Vernon from California, where they were part of the same church. They were living in the Los Angeles area when Vernon was politically squeezed into retirement along with retiring chief Daryl Gates. Because of his storied career, Bob seemed the logical choice to succeed Gates as LAPD Chief. However, his career was callously stained at its closing by people who lacked appreciation for his Christian convictions and high standards, as well as for his commitment to not playing political games. Those who knew him, however, knew that he was a man of integrity and honor, and were troubled at watching the attempts to trash his brilliant career.

Cheryl and the Rubeys met with Vernon in Mayor Coles office for an hour, then attended an evening session at which one hundred fifty officers and spouses met to hear his address. He candidly spoke that night about the cop—his character, behavior, and attitudes. He challenged his listeners to be right in their work and their homes, and above all be willing to stand up for God as an important part of their lives. At the end of the session, several rose to their feet to publicly declare their intention to do so. It was encouraging to see evidence of this kind of heart within the law enforcement family.

The following day Vernon presented a daylong ethics seminar for officers that was very beneficial to all who were able to participate. His many years of police life and service provide him a unique credibility in his promotions of integrity among these professionals.

During the early weeks after Mark's death, Cheryl found herself in a roller-coaster emotional state. She felt strong in some areas, but weak in others; from all appearances, though, she appeared to be handling things remarkably well. She did say, however, that her "world was upside down." Consequently, she didn't wait long to begin packing away Mark's things, because they brought emotional pain every time she saw them. She painted and redecorated the girls' rooms, bought a few pieces of furniture, and began remodeling her kitchen. These projects helped her stay occupied, which helped distract her from the constant emotional pain.

A security system was donated and installed to give her and the girls added safety. Firemen volunteered to install a sprinkler system, and a local door company donated a new garage door for her home. Many of the things Mark had wanted to do, but lacked the money and time to accomplish, were done or initiated soon after his death. By doing these things Cheryl both assuaged the pain of his absence and also completed some of what he would eventually have done had he lived. In her heart, she felt she was doing these things for him as much as for her and the girls.

Early in November of 1997, Bill Cosby was scheduled to be in Boise for a one-night show. The Rubeys had purchased tickets as soon as they became available so that their family could spend an evening together enjoying the lovable Cosby. It was also planned as part of an early birthday present for Mark's thirtieth birthday a week later.

On the night of Cosby's Boise appearance, it had been but seven weeks since Mark's death. The family had lost enthusiasm for the event, but at the last moment they decided to go and see if they could release some of the heavy sorrow they had been carrying. There was an added downside to the show—it was being held in the Boise State University Pavilion, the exact location of Mark's funeral. This would their first time back in the building since the funeral. That factor alone nearly kept them from going, because they were still very tender about exposing themselves to the pain of what had gone on there a few weeks earlier.

Once they decided to go, arrangements were made for them to be included in a pre-show meeting with Bill Cosby. They ended up last in a line of some seventy-five people who would have opportunity to personally meet him and obtain autographs. Since Cosby had himself endured the calamitous experience of the murder of his son, Enis, ten months earlier in Los Angeles, the family felt that a video of Mark's funeral might possibly have some meaning to him because of what he had gone through.

As would be expected, Cosby cracked jokes with the people in line as they advanced to where he was signing autographs. When Cheryl finally reached him, she placed the video on the table before him. As he looked down at the tape, she briefly explained that her husband was the policeman killed in Boise a few weeks earlier, and that since he had recently lost a son he might find Mark's funeral service meaningful for his own comfort. Cosby instantly stopped joking and responded to Cheryl seriously.

"And how is it with you and God?" he asked. It was a very unexpected response.

"Good," she answered. "God has given me grace and strength to get through this and we're on good terms."

"That's good to hear," he said, "because, you know, many people get mad at God over things like this." His words encouraged Cheryl and the family. The show that followed, while hard to fully enjoy because of its lightness, did help the family shed the grip of sorrow for a while.

A few days later came November 17, 1997—the date that would have been Mark's thirtieth birthday. Knowing that this would be an especially hard day for Cheryl, the Rubeys took her and the girls to the neighboring community of Nampa to wander through the antique shops. Cheryl wanted something to occupy her mind and keep her focus off the meaning of this day as much as possible and for as long as possible. This would have been a big day in their lives together had he been still living.

Late in the afternoon, Cheryl and the girls decided to purchase balloons to take to the grave. When they exited the store, each had a balloon in hand—the girls each had a heart-shape, and Cheryl's was black with lips all over it and the words, "I love you." These really weren't what they wanted, but were the best ones they could find. Arnold watched them cross the parking lot to where he waited in the car, and could not help but weep at what he was watching. "This is crazy," he thought. "Balloons for a grave? This isn't even real." How empty this was for Cheryl and the girls, but then again, there was little if anything that could give any better meaning to this sad occasion. At least the balloons could grace the grave for a while.

At the gravesite each fastened her balloon to the iron cross that had identified Mark's grave since its removal from the site of the shooting. The cemetery had granted permission to place the cross there until the headstone would be ready, some months later. It was painful to witness—balloons blowing gaily in the wind, tied to a grave marker. A mere two months had passed since September 20, and it seemed that this family was already living in another world and another time.

The following day the Rubeys hosted the first of what became monthly Law Enforcement Fellowships in their home. This was an informal Bible study and discussion time for officers and spouses, with child-care at a neighbor's home. They had talked of doing this for a year, but when Mark's death occurred, they knew they were meant to move forward with personal involvement.

A handful of couples came to that first meeting. Cheryl felt a need to be a part of this gathering, and was also there that first night. It was hard on her—as she watched each couple leave together, she quickly became very depressed that she had to go home alone. It painfully reminded her that everything in her life, even her relationship to the police department, was undergoing unsolicited change.

Jonelle and Julia moved in and out of struggling over being without their daddy. When Cheryl sensed that they were hurting, she would get Mark's picture and sit down with them to talk about it. She encouraged them to talk to their daddy about what was on their hearts, and this process seemed to bring relief to them.

The extent of their hurt showed up at a pre-Christmas "Birthday Party for Jesus" to which both girls were invited. They were part of a group of seventeen children at their Sunday school teacher's home. Most of the group were girls, and at some point during the gathering

Julia asked one of them, "Do you have a daddy?" to which the girl replied, "Yes."

Julia then said, "I don't have a daddy. My daddy's in heaven."

After this, she went to every girl and asked, "Do you have a daddy?" All said yes, until one girl told her, "I have two daddies."

"You have two daddies?" Julia asked. "I don't have one. Could I have one of yours?"

One evening sometime later, Cheryl and the girls were at her parents' home for a meal. As was often done at mealtime, one of them would be asked if she would like to pray for the meal. Julia volunteered this night and as she prayed, she moved everyone to somber silence. After thanking God for several things, including the food, she closed her prayer with a sudden shift of thoughts to her father. "Help Daddy not to get killed again...to get a bullet in his shirt."

Jonelle, though only six, seemed to possess an uncanny sense of trust in God's purposes in spite of what had been taken from her. Her Sunday school teacher, Esther Crandell, a woman in her late seventies who had just become a new widow herself a few months earlier, was still teaching children, and had a special relationship with these girls. She arranged some time with Jo one day just to be with her and to comfort her in the loss of her daddy. At an appropriate time, Esther asked Jo if she was upset at God for allowing her daddy to die. She immediately responded, "Why should I be mad at God? He just wanted my daddy to be in heaven with Him." Esther later shared that Jo became her comforter that day instead of the other way around.

In December both the Police Department and the City of Boise honored Mark as the Officer of the Year. At the Mayor's annual Christmas party, Captain Mike Prynch of the Boise Police Department shared privately that he had just completed two weeks reviewing this case intensely. He stated that the shooting was "extremely frightening" to the officers, and that in some ways they may never get over the feeling of trauma they experienced. This was a sobering perspective. Not only was the Stall family deeply affected, but the police family as well. This was an event that would leave lifelong scars on a great many people.

In May 1998, twenty-five members of the Stall/Rubey family attended the National Law Enforcement Memorial Observance in Washington D.C. They were accompanied by Officer Rob Berrier from the Boise Police Department and his wife Amy. Rob was Mark's partner on the night of his death. They all participated in several days of events sponsored by C.O.P.S. (Concerns Of Police Survivors). The events included a candlelight vigil at the National Law Enforcement Memorial in Judiciary Square, seminar sessions for survivors of police deaths, and the Memorial service at the Capitol on May 15. Mark's name was read at the vigil on May 13, and again at the Capitol when Cheryl was escorted by Rob to place a carnation in Mark's memory in a huge police badge of flowers. It was a gathering of grievers from across the nation and provinces of the United States. One hundred seventy-one names were read, including one hundred sixty from 1997 and eleven additions from previous years. It was humbling and comforting to mingle with so many sorrowful families who were also going through the loss of a loved one in the line of duty in 1997. Some survivors from previous years also returned to again be part of this gathering.

Among many special events that week, two particular ones stand out. The first involved U.S. Senator Dirk Kempthorne from Idaho (now Governor of Idaho). In his conference room in the Senate wing, he graciously gave nearly an hour to the family for questions, pictures, and an explanation of what he would be doing on the floor of the Senate that week. For the fifth consecutive year, and now the final year necessary, a resolution would be presented on the floor of the Senate declaring May 15 as a national memorial day for fallen officers. Senator Kempthorne would soon read this resolution on the Senate floor once again, as he had done each of the previous four years. Thereafter, it would be a regular observance by law. It is of interest historically that Mark's death was an integral part of Senator Kempthorne's presentation to the Senate for this final reading. (See the full text of Senator Kempthorne's resolution in the Appendix).

The second event involved Greg Casey, Sergeant at Arms of the U.S. Senate, who requested to meet with the family. Greg is from Boise, and had been deeply moved by Mark's slaying, though he was now living in Washington. As all twenty-five of the Stall family, and also the Berriers, crammed into his office, he addressed them in tears. He told them he considered it a privilege to meet this family, for he had taken a special interest in Mark's death and had watched the funeral on television. He had in fact been so moved that, at his December 1997 gathering of the Capitol Police force, he spoke of Mark's death as a challenge to his own officers. When he finished his remarks, he gave a signed copy of his speech to Cheryl for a keep-sake.

The meeting with Greg Casey preceded by two and a half months the shocking shooting deaths of two officers at the Capitol in late July 1998. They were the first two Capitol Police officers in United States history to die on duty. They were part of Greg's contingent of officers, and added two more indelible scars to his heart along with that from Mark Stall. It was an unpleasant new chapter in the life of America. The National Peace Officers' Memorial, located in the shadow of the Capitol, would now add the names of national peacekeepers who died doing their duty. It reflects the spiral of violence that is growing ever more prevalent in our nation.

Life cannot ever be the same for families like the Stalls. Most homes and lives continue on as usual in spite of how they are touched by the deaths of others; but in certain homes and families, life can never return to what it once was. The present and future must be faced under immutably transformed circumstances.

Cheryl Stall certainly faced an uncertain future; one that could not be adequately reshaped except by God Himself. What would it hold? No one could know at that time what lay ahead, but God was about to bring about yet another extraordinary occurrence in Cheryl's life for which the community and the rest of the family were quite unprepared.

15

Courtney

When Mark died, Cheryl at first wondered if happiness would ever again come to her. She had no way of knowing how long the pain of grief would continue to overshadow her life. At the time it seemed that only darkness lay ahead.

How does a young widow go about getting back on her feet? What hardships and difficulties lie ahead? What were her little girls actually going through in their childlike experiences, and what would they have to deal with in the future because of this? Was there meant to be another man in her life, and another daddy for her girls?

Many could not help but think about what the future might hold for this young widow. People tried to sense in some degree what it must be like to have to deal with what she now had to deal with in her life. Many made comments such as , "I've tried to think what it would be like to be without my husband or wife." To try to sense such a thing as this is natural but unrealistic, because while one can attempt to imagine how empty it would be, in the next instant he or she can revert back to knowing their spouse is in reality still there. Cheryl could not. Her nightmare never disappeared; it always remained. The only reality she had was that Mark was truly gone. She could not return to normalcy, even for a moment.

She incessantly had to come to terms with how to live without her husband and how to nurture her children through the grief process. Thankfully, many provided financial assistance, and other kinds of help were also supplied. She had accumulated enough resources so that she could give full attention to trying to put their lives back together. Even so, in the first few weeks and months she struggled to find some sense of wholeness. A huge gap in their lives had to be closed through God's healing processes.

Months later, when she felt she could more objectively face and talk about the future, she began sharing her evolving thoughts about remarriage with her parents and a few other people in whom she felt she could confide. They all supported her in the ideas she had structured about her future, but most also felt that her expectations were loftier than what reality would actually provide for her. But she did not waver, in spite of their stated opinions that she might be setting her goals beyond reasonable expectations.

First, she strongly felt that she did not want to date. She disliked the prospect of "looking for husband-material," and did not want to go through that kind of process. Dating, she felt, was fraught with dangers for someone in her situation. She was much too fragile to be seriously going out with anyone, and simply did not want to contend with the insecurities of dating.

Second, she did not want to consider a man who was coming out of a divorce as a future husband. She felt he would bring the baggage of a broken relationship into the new marriage, and she would in turn give him the baggage of dealing with her unique problems because of the involuntary severance of her marriage through death. Because of the nature of what she had gone through, she felt the compatibility factor would just be too challenging with this kind of union.

Third, she wanted a future husband to be a Christian man who shared the same kind of commitment to Christ that she did. She wanted a strong spiritual leader for both her and her girls as they moved on with their lives. She and Mark had grown a lot together in spiritual life, and she desired to continue that process with a new husband.

Fourth, she desired a husband and father for her children who would share her parenting perspective. She and Mark had committed themselves to raising their family in a biblical manner, and had in fact completed a parenting course for the second time. She felt she needed a husband who would gladly continue what she and Mark had begun.

Fifth, she strongly felt a future husband would have to understand grief in order to understand her. This meant he would have had to go through some kind of grieving himself. A man who had not tasted sorrow in his life would not likely be as sensitive to what she would continue to go through for some time to come. While this seemed a most unusual requirement for a marriage, it did make sense. She knew she would have some degree of sorrow for the rest of her life, as would her girls in future years. A new husband and dad would need to be sensitive to this dimension of struggle in all of them.

These five things, each individually important to Cheryl, now became her collective criteria for any future relationship. To find all these ingredients in one man without some kind of dating process seemed highly unlikely, yet she honestly felt it could and would be a viable possibility when the time was right for her to be serious about anyone.

In August 1997, one month before Mark's death, Cheryl's long-time college friend Dr. Carol Powers had informed her that her brother's wife in Ohio had just been diagnosed with stomach cancer. She asked that Cheryl and Mark remember them in prayer, for they faced an uncertain future. Robin Chamberlain was only thirty-two years of age, and the cancer was already stage four when diagnosed.

When Cheryl's world came apart on that September morning a month later, she was instantly cut off from the progression of Robin's situation in Ohio. She would remain so until January, when Carol called and told her that Robin had passed away. She said her brother could use some encouragement, as it had been a trying ordeal. Robin had been away from her home a considerable amount of time for treatments, then isolated much of the time once home because of her condition. Cheryl agreed to send him a note.

Carol thought that her brother, Courtney, might not respond to Cheryl at this point in time, but that it wouldn't hurt to at least try to provide him with some comforting and encouraging words. He did respond, however, by e-mailing Cheryl an expressive note thanking her for her thoughtful words to him. He shared with her that God had been his strong comforter through all that he and his four daughters had experienced, but that the pain of Robin's suffering and death had also been great.

It was the beginning of an ongoing exchange of communications between them. They also began to open up more and more with each other about what they had experienced in their respective situations, sharing what it was like to cope with all the aspects of their ordeals. They discovered how much the other had loved and still did love their missing spouse. Cheryl spoke to Courtney about how much she missed Mark, and Courtney shared the depth of his loss of Robin. They cried together, and encouraged each other in turn in nurturing and sustaining the memory of their loved one. Both were enduring hard days and nights.

Eventually questions began to emerge about the future. Do you plan to remarry some day? If so, how soon do you feel that could be for you? Do you plan to stay in the same city and house, or are the memories too painful? What do you sense your girls need at this time? Are you struggling with parenting alone? E-mail after e-mail, phone call after phone call, they kept asking each other these and other questions.

They each began thinking the other might possibly be the one God meant to be part of rebuilding their lives and homes. They shared a kindred spirit in many ways, and also shared a mutual desire to make and keep God central in their lives. Even at this stage of their now-evolving interest in one another for the future, neither had even seen a picture of the other. Their developing attraction was completely without physical considerations, and was based solely on what they had been learning about each other long-distance. Another very important factor was that they were each independently asking God to shape their relationship into something more permanent, if that was what He wanted.

By the spring of 1998, Cheryl told a couple of friends, then her parents, that she and Courtney had been discussing marriage. Arnold and Kay recoiled and told her they felt she was being too hasty. In their opinion, she was not through the worst of her grieving, nor was she ready to assume the responsibility of a new family. Courtney had four daughters ranging from two to eleven, and Cheryl was still struggling at times with her two. To add four more children plus a new husband was a huge step to take. On top of it, she had not yet even met Courtney! What if she found she didn't feel as drawn to him in person as she had long-distance? What if he didn't feel the same toward her after meeting her?

This prospect of marriage concerned Arnold so much that it strained his relationship with his daughter. She became increasingly convinced this was the right thing for her and the girls, while he was concerned that it was just too soon. He avoided talking about the subject, and she quietly brooded over his resistance. In the meanwhile, she and Courtney continued to correspond, talk by phone, and plan for the future.

In the spring, Cheryl informed her folks that she was going to Michigan to spend a few days with her friend Carol Powers, Courtney's sister. During that time she would meet Courtney for the first time. Again it seemed too soon, yet if they were seriously considering marriage, they certainly needed to meet and see if this prospect would continue to hold up after they became acquainted in person. Cheryl flew to Ohio, where Courtney met her at the airport and drove them to his sister's home a few hours north. When Cheryl boarded the plane to return to Boise a few days later, she had a ring on her finger.

Upon her return, she said that Courtney was all she expected and more. She was even more confident that their pending marriage was meant to be, and assured her parents that when they met Courtney they would understand why she felt about him the way she did. Courtney's parents were excited also about the prospect of their son marrying Cheryl, since they had already met her three years earlier when she had been part of Carol's wedding in Ohio. In addition, Carol had been talking up Cheryl to the entire family, and felt certain she would be great for her brother. The relationship was gaining a full head of steam.

In early May Courtney flew to Boise to meet Cheryl's family and to look over the area. He already had in mind that if he and Cheryl were meant to be together, it was to be in Boise, not in Ohio. Upon his arrival at the Boise airport, he experienced the prankster side of Cheryl. He had been made aware that she could be mischievous on occasion, but he didn't know the extent to which she might go. She had arranged with Lori Sperry, a Boise police officer, to be party to a ploy she had in mind for Courtney. As he stepped into the concourse he didn't see Cheryl, but he did see Lori in uniform. He did not know Lori, and he knew nothing was wrong in respect to himself, so he suspected nothing.

Lori immediately approached him (Cheryl cued her from out of sight so she would get the right man) and asked him to step over to the nearest wall. She then asked him to turn around, face the wall, and put his hands behind him. He thought this strange, but since he was unsure of what was going on, he readily complied. As Lori slapped handcuffs on him, she exclaimed, "Welcome to Boise!" Cheryl was fortunate that Courtney didn't get back on the plane and terminate this relationship then and there!

He stayed with the Rubeys, and they all began their mutual acquaintance. They talked for several hours during the course of his stay, and candidly confronted the concerns and questions they all were dealing with. One of the big questions was how he would feel about coming into the eye of the needle—living in the shadow of Mark Stall. Moving to Boise would force him to find acceptance among the many people who had loved and respected Mark. He would have to compete with the maintaining of Mark's memory, and would be forced to live with all the things associated with his death. Did these possibilities not intimidate him to a certain degree?

He admitted that these things were concerns, but said he had no intention of competing with Mark, for that would be impossible and unnecessary. Mark was special to his family and to his community, and nothing should diminish that bond. His marriage to Cheryl would not change that in any way, as far as he was concerned. He shared that he would even like to be part of remembering Mark. When asked if he might tire of hearing about Mark Stall, he replied that he had no control over that aspect of things and would just have to deal with it if and when it became a problem. But most importantly, what the Rubeys discovered during Courtney's visit was that he was indeed the quality person Cheryl had said he was. They liked what they saw in Courtney.

While in Boise, Courtney also attended Cheryl's church, and found that the people who loved Mark would also open their hearts to him. It was awkward for them at first, not knowing him, but to their credit they made him feel welcome and wanted. And to Courtney's credit, he walked into their fellowship with a humble and brave heart. Cheryl was allowed to introduce him to the congregation, after which he spoke to them about the loss of his wife and God's grace to them through that time. He resolutely thanked them for what they had done for Cheryl and her girls, then expressed that it was his desire to please the Lord with his own life. Those present were favorably impressed with his thoughts and expressions. It was one additional step in providing acceptance and appreciation for Cheryl's future husband.

A few days later, while her parents were visiting Colonial Williamsburg, Cheryl informed them by phone that she and Courtney were planning to be married in late June. "Why so soon?" she was asked. She replied that they had been weighing everything related to their situations—things such as helping the six girls get acquainted before school started in the fall and getting established in their Boise home before school began—and it just seemed that this timing would work best in regard to the many factors involved in this complex new union.

She then asked her dad, "Will you marry us?" He replied that he would, but again expressed his concerns that he felt it was too soon. He still thought she would be better off to wait until at least the first anniversary of Mark's death, so that all the "firsts" would be behind her. She felt, however, that she needed and wanted Courtney to go through the death anniversary with her; that with his help she would be better able emotionally to get through that time.

Cheryl broke the news to Ray and Nancy Stall a few days later in Washington D.C. They and others of their family had come to Washington for the National Police Week 1998. Ray and Nancy graciously accepted that Cheryl needed to move on with her life, but it was extremely difficult to think about the shift from their son to another man this soon. It was providential, however, that this news came while they were all together in seminar sessions at the Concerns Of Police Survivors (C.O.P.S) in Alexandria, Virginia, May 13-16, 1998.

As the different family members attended specialized sessions for survivors of law enforcement deaths and listened to story after story of death and heartache in officers' families across America, they were also introduced to the ongoing turmoil in some of these families. In the aftermath of some of these deaths, it was not uncommon to hear of heightened animosity between in-laws and of serious relational separations. The Stalls soon gained a new and special appreciation for the relationship they continued to hold with Cheryl and her two girls. They were not angry and fighting with one another, and they were always welcome in her home. Cheryl loved Mark, and she also loved them. She assured them that she would always love their son who had been her husband for eight years. To her, remarrying did not mean she was going to forget Mark, but that she was going on and building further what she and Mark had begun together. She believed this was what Mark would want for her and the girls for their future.

The eye-opening experience of seeing the downside of unpleasant relational situations readily changed the Stalls' perspective—they knew they had been and still were very blessed by the strong bond they had with Cheryl. From that point on they accepted the changes, in spite of the difficulty of letting go of the past.

Another confirmation of the step Cheryl was taking came from a family member who said that Mark had talked about this to him. He revealed that Mark had candidly told him that if anything ever happened to him, he would want Cheryl to consider remarriage soon afterwards. It was a concern to him that she find a daddy—the right daddy—for his girls. He did not want any of them to be very long without the support of a loving husband and father.

The wedding was set for Saturday, June 27, 1998 in Marietta, Ohio. The outdoor ceremony was to be held in the large and beautiful yard of an old Chamberlain family home located on Chamberlain Drive. Courtney, the seventh of ten children, selected this meaningful family setting for the occasion. It was to be a smaller wedding by design, perhaps eighty people. It almost had to be moved indoors, as heavy rains pelted the region the night before and continued until half an hour before the scheduled ceremony; but the rain let up just in time, and just long enough, to allow the ceremony and reception to be held outdoors as planned. A few hours after the wedding, a tornado came through Marietta and surrounding areas, and flooding occurred throughout southern Ohio.

As Courtney and Cheryl stepped in turn through the rose garden trellis with six girls surrounding them, they looked upon seven parents seated within the encirclement of rose bushes: Harold and Elizabeth Chamberlain, Arnold and Kay Rubey, Ray and Nancy Stall, and Sharon Corban, Courtney's deceased wife's mother. Fred Corban was unable to attend because of a family illness. It was an amazing sight—all the parents of the bride and groom, and three of the four parents of the deceased spouses—all in support of this union. Ray and Nancy Stall had driven all the way from California to Ohio to witness the wedding of their daughter-in-law to the man who would become their granddaughters' new daddy. It was an awesome display of class on their part, as well as for Sharon Corban, whose daughter had been gone but five months.

Courtney personally seated all four mothers, after which Cheryl walked alone down a sidewalk from the old house and through the trellis. The six girls had already taken their places for the ceremony.

As Cheryl came toward him to stand in the spot where she would exchange vows with Courtney, Arnold struggled to contain his emotions. Her walk down that path without an escort had a very special meaning to Cheryl, as they had emotionally learned from her the evening before. At that time, during an informal rehearsal, Arnold asked her if she would like him to walk her down the sidewalk aisle.

"You already walked me once," she softly replied.

"I know," he replied, "but I'll walk you again."

She stood in silence for a moment as tears welled up in her eyes and coursed down her cheeks. Then, again in a soft whisper, she said, "Mark is walking me down the aisle."

Everyone lost it—they could not restrain their tears from joining with hers.

After Arnold read a poem requested by Courtney and Cheryl, the song "Blessing in the Thorn" was sung, to describe what the circumstances of this wedding really were. As a result, Arnold was unable to begin his remarks—he was too emotional to speak. His struggle was representative of everyone present. Cheryl and Courtney, more than any, knew the pain and joy that were mixed together at this moment. They, too, stood with their eyes full of tears.

It was apparent that this ceremony could not begin in joy, but first had to bridge sorrow. When Arnold could finally speak, he shakily said, "Today, in this place, under unique circumstances not even remotely thought possible a year ago, several families related to those circumstances, along with numerous friends, gather to witness a new union of two people who have passed through deep sorrows.

"Cheryl and Courtney, you both once before entered a union in which you each promised yourself to another for a lifetime. You have each also watched the one to whom you promised that love have his and her own lifetime cut short by tragedy and disease. Because of those circumstances, and because of God's mysterious providence in bringing you together in the aftermath, you meet today at this altar as a widow and a widower.

"You have new love while yet loving your dear one gone. You have a new companionship while always holding a place in the room of your heart for the one who has gone before you into heaven. You have been through a hard season; may God be pleased to give you a long season of pleasantness ahead.

"This is a bittersweet gathering. Mark and Robin are deeply missed. None of us can or will easily forget the gripping pain of yesterday, but we all know we need and yearn for the renewed joy today can bring. So now, by God's enabling grace, we all join you, Courtney and Cheryl, in looking ahead in joy. These precious girls have a daddy and a mommy who love God, and they once again have the warmth of a complete and loving family structure. How you love each other will perpetuate the legacies of Mark and Robin, the daddy and mommy they loved and still love."

At the conclusion of the ceremony, Courtney spoke to the gathered crowd about the sacrifices Mark and Robin had made in their deaths. As he held four beautiful bouquets before them, he explained what those bouquets symbolized. The pink rose in each bouquet represented the perfecting of love that he and Cheryl would strive to achieve; the red rose, "the love we had"; the blue ribbon "what Mark lived for and died for"; and the red ribbon, "Robin's courage in fighting cancer." He then presented a like bouquet to all four mothers. They had bridged the past to the future.

They honeymooned in Hawaii for five days, then returned to Ohio to begin packing up the Chamberlain home for the move to Idaho. The six girls were now one household, and the challenges of sibling adjustments began. For two months they played and cried together, and for two months Courtney and Cheryl packed up the house. In mid-August, Courtney ended his ten-year career at the computer company where he had worked. It was a difficult goodbye, but he felt confident that his decision to go to Idaho was the right one.

Ten days later they pulled out of Marietta, Ohio with a U-Haul truck, a Blazer, a Suburban, and six girls. Cheryl's purchase of an eight-passenger Suburban after Mark's death was ideal for the new family. She obtained the vehicle with some of the funds that had been provided, because she and Mark had often talked about getting a new Suburban someday. In the terribly emotional aftermath of his death, she bought it for him as well as for her and the girls. Now, it was the perfect vehicle to transport her new family across the country.

They pushed hard and arrived in Boise after three very long days of travel.

The Stall three were now the Chamberlain eight, starting a new life in Boise, Idaho.

16

Perspectives On Law Enforcement

Mark Stall was a good police officer, and well trained. He was alert and observant to what was going on around him, and he was careful about the conducting of his work. He chose law enforcement as a career because he felt a calling to police work and because he believed he could do a good job. To him, the job went beyond "catching" evil-doers and law-breakers—he wanted to help initiate change in those with more serious problems, and to encourage them to turn their lives in a better direction if they had the desire and will to do so. This attitude characterized his few years with the departments he served. If it were possible to locate and then interview the individuals or families who had contact with Mark, they would likely describe him as one officer who treated them respectfully. He was professional, and attempted to do his job the way it was meant to be done.

Not all officers cut it as straight as Mark Stall, even in Boise. He was not without flaws, but he worked at doing right. His name and reputation were important to him, as was the reputation of the police department he represented and in which he served. While he was proud to be a Boise officer, he did not want to be perceived as a cocky cop with an attitude.

Some officers do have an air, an arrogance, an intoxication with the authority that comes with their position. These individuals rub some citizens the wrong way by the way they deal with or handle them, and they more readily attract resentment from those who simply do not care for cops in the first place. Swagger, however, does not make a cop an evil person or guilty of misconduct. On the other hand, officers who demonstrate unprofessional behaviors show their moral weaknesses more so than their pride. On occasion, some are found to be professionally careless or even ill motivated. Those traits will surface, and those who are cocky and mouthy will have that conduct called into question by their police department. They will either change for good or eventually be fired. In contrast are the vast majority of officers, who responsibly do their jobs as guardians over the welfare of the community. As such, they should be respected for their higher-risk work.

Boise, and undoubtedly other communities like it, have vocal minorities of anti-authoritarian people who manage to obtain airtime and column space to malign the police department whenever possible. They seem to want the community to distrust their police, and they further want officers involved in serious incidents to be disparaged before the public and disciplined by the department, whether or not they deserve such discipline. These voices also seem to find a way to excuse the perpetrators and automatically assign blame to the police for how the situation turned out. They give the impression that they believe a conspiracy exists among officers to deliberately maltreat or even do away with certain individuals for no apparent reason. Some portray the police as legal assassins with a Gestapo mentality who carelessly wield the power behind their guns and badges.

It would seem unnecessary to have to state that there are many persons at large in society with savage motives who also carry weapons, legal or illegal, with which they initiate actions against policemen or citizens. Some utilize vehicles and even bombs. Some of these individuals, when confronted by the police, resist with such belligerence that officers are forced to use physical restraints or other needful force to make them comply. However, to the defense of the lawbreaker now leap those who, although not present at the incident, nevertheless excuse those whom the police confronted and proceed to condemn the officers for taking action against them. This inside-out logic, furthered by anti-police public statements, often results in further knee-jerk reactions from the public. Even civic leaders, who ought to be strong supporters of their police departments, find themselves remaining silent or questioning their police so as to appear more open-minded.

In our kind of society, unless it is blatantly obvious that the police were in error, they should be trusted or given the benefit of the doubt until it is proven that their position lacks credibility. Most law-breakers seldom admit to wrongdoing; rather, they loudly proclaim that they couldn't possibly be guilty of what they've been accused. That would then mean that the police had no reason to confront them and were picking on them without good cause. It's the bad, bad police department again, doing their authoritarian thing against innocent citizens.

On the other hand, if an officer is found guilty of misconduct in the course of his work, he should bear the consequences of his actions. However, it must be adequately proven, not assumed, that he is guilty of wrongdoing before his integrity is impugned.

Some individuals seem quite willing to voice toleration for aberrant behavior, while at the same time expressing intolerance for those commissioned to lawfully deal with wayward behavior. Even the courts seem to lack the resolve to clamp down on certain evildoers when it is justified. The result is that society slowly and unwittingly narrows the gap of distinction between good and evil. Those standing for right are brought lower, as though they were the bad people, and those doing ill are promoted as not so bad. The losers in this jaded kind of thinking are those on the side of law and order, for they have the most to lose. An old adage is fitting: When truth compromises with error, it is always truth that gives up something, because error had nothing to begin with. Paraphrased and adapted to this context we could say: When right compromises with wrong, it is right that gives up something, because wrong had nothing to begin with.

The Bible contains many warnings about good and evil. Since the Scriptures have given nations a foundation for societal laws and responsible behavior throughout history, they are surely worthwhile standards that would still benefit society today. What we lack today are minds that are willing to take such warnings seriously. For example:

Proverbs 18:5, "It is not good to show partiality to the wicked, or to overthrow the righteous in judgment."

Proverbs 17:15, "He who justifies the wicked, and he who condemns the just, both of them alike are an abomination to the Lord."

Proverbs 28:4, "Those who forsake the law (the spiritual laws of God) praise the wicked, but such as keep the law contend with them."

Malachi 2:17, "...In what way have we wearied Him (the Lord): In that you say, 'Everyone who does evil is good in the sight of the Lord, and He delights in them'...."

Isaiah 5:20, "Woe to those who call evil good, and good evil; who put darkness for light, and light for darkness; who put bitter for sweet, and sweet for bitter!"

Ecclesiastes 5:8 speaks to "...the violent perversion of justice and righteousness in a province...."

As far as God is concerned, it is morally reprehensible to excuse wrongdoers. To then go still further and categorically blame those asked to protect us from the ills of society only adds more distortion. As long as societies, including our own, continue to reject proven divine mandates, good and decent people will bear the brunt of injustice, and law enforcement personnel will continue to die in record numbers confronting those allowed to perpetrate their foul deeds. Through the excesses of permissive society and the leniency of the courts, the cancer of wickedness will continue to proliferate. Instead of rooting out the cancer, we allow it to remain by both ignoring and excusing its severity.

The most effective solution to help stem the upward spiral of wrongdoing is to initiate immediate and serious crackdowns on felonious crimes, followed with harsh consequences. In respect to law officers, to deliberately or with malice kill a policeman would automatically mean the death penalty. Period. We already have laws on the books in some states with severe penalties or capital punishment for such crimes, but the resolve to impose full punishment is lacking. Unfortunately, even if drastic steps like these were instituted now, it would still require significant time to effectively move our world toward true justice and more peaceable living. We have already allowed it to get too far out of hand.

God likewise counsels governments to practice swift justice as a deterrent to crime. When punishment is slow or delayed, the consequences are passed back into the community itself. Ecclesiastes 8:11 explains how: "Because the sentence against an evil work is not executed speedily, therefore the heart of the sons of men is fully set to do evil." Isaiah 26:10 provides still another perspective about the mindset of evildoers: "Let grace be shown to the wicked, yet he will not learn righteousness; in the land of uprightness he will deal unjustly...."

What is the bottom line here? Those who disrespect and disregard the law will continue in that pattern until they are internally changed, or are punished according to the actual severity of their crimes.

Few people these days, including government officials themselves, understand the basic and needful purposes of government. Its prime purpose is not to provide handout programs or develop entitlements as broadly as possible; rather, it is to be responsible for the provision of peacekeepers for the citizens. Nationally this peacekeeping function is provided through the military; on a state, county, or city level it is provided through the police. When taxes are collected from the citizens to provide services in their behalf, an appropriate portion of those monies should first and foremost be earmarked for law enforcement. Why? Because people with evil hearts, whether local or international, always have a presence that requires enforcement of some kind in order to adequately protect the people. This is the kind of world we live in.

Therefore, the business of state or local government is to help *prevent crime* by providing a law enforcement presence, *control crime* by providing an adequate number of peacekeepers, and *restrain crime* by allowing policemen to properly enforce the law. Beyond this, courts are needed with the authority and the resolve to enforce punishment equal to the crimes committed.

The lack of proper implementation of law enforcement is even causing some smaller towns in a few western states and parts of the East Coast to abolish their police departments. They are instead looking to County Sheriff's Departments to do the policing for them.

In September 1997, the month Mark was killed, one New York community took steps in the opposite direction—they abolished their police department through their Town Board. When the issue was later put to a vote, the citizens affirmed the Board's decision by a margin of greater than two to one. The reason for eliminating their police? Lower taxes. The lowered tax base without police protection will, however, almost undoubtedly open the door to new community problems and increased crime. This community will become an example of how tax-driven decision-making can provide evildoers unrestricted freedom to ply their trades, once the restraints to their activities have been removed.

Eventually the citizens will begin clamoring for protection, when they have found out the hard way the degree to which bad elements will permeate their domain. They will find that tax savings, however attractive to their pocketbooks, do not deter those with other things on their minds. Lawless people will find this community a pleasant pasture, with fewer eyes to watch what they do. The only unknown thing is to what degree the community will be ravaged.

Although some might view this as overly cynical, national statistics confirm that serious crimes are continuing to escalate nationwide. In increasing numbers of places, existing jails and prisons are already unable to accommodate the number of criminals who have been convicted. Murderers log long years on death row on the backs of the taxpayers while endless appeals go on. If we don't pay for law enforcement at the front end by providing adequate peacekeepers, we will surely pay on the back end by building more and more expensive prisons to accommodate more and more criminals. Sadly, things are not improving—the trend toward evil is alive and well.

Those who are middle-aged and older probably remember growing up with a healthy respect for law enforcement. Policemen were viewed as good guys and may have been friends and neighbors. We trusted them and felt more protected because they were present in our communities. Things have not really changed over the years; as a matter of fact, today police are needed even more because of our expanding population. Their job remains the protection of citizens and the providing of a presence that enforces law and order in every community. It is alarming, though, that while we have more police than ever, there is also more crime than ever. Some of that trend is due to increased questioning of law enforcement departments and a diminishing of the role and worth of our law-keepers. In addition, we have grown so soft in exacting proper punishment for grave crimes that evildoers do not feel constrained from committing serious criminal acts.

Even veteran police officers look at today's law enforcement differently than they once did. Some have indicated that if they were starting out in a new career today, they would be unlikely to choose law enforcement based on what they now experience within law enforcement. So much has changed in what is expected of the modern officer and in respect to the protected rights of those they confront daily, that they wonder if it is worth the strain they endure to do the job right. These perceptions are not based on an unwillingness to improve or change areas of police procedures that need improvement, but on a general basis. The person caught in the clear commission of a crime seems to have just as good a chance to beat the rap as the officer has to make it stick, because quite often the officer is questioned and made out to have mishandled the situation. Then, to add insult to injury, the lawbreaker walks. Police officers can't help but wonder how much they are truly accomplishing in trying to clean up the community when being called on technicalities and having the tables turned on them is the order of the day.

When situations arise in which a policeman is required to use physical force or his gun in order to protect himself or to subdue a transgressor, he or she is likely to end up facing some kind of litigation because of having used force. The police are increasingly expected to endure more, as lawbreakers are allowed to get away with more. Good and evil are now on more equal terms; good is not necessarily better than evil when weighed legally. It has become a matter of which one can outdo the other in legal maneuvering and come out the victor.

The constant questioning and second-guessing that follows police incidents only adds further difficulty to the ability of field officers to feel free to approach their job in the same manner thereafter. They feel even more restraint, or even hesitancy, which may make them more tentative in facing lethal situations. Those who do not know what police officers face on the streets of most American cities, yet roundly criticize the way they respond to dangerous situations, lack real understanding of the dangers these brave officers face. Were they in the shoes of an officer facing what they occasionally do, they would likely do as any cautious officer does in order to protect himself or others. The bottom line is that there are those on our streets who would cause harm, using weapons or other methods. Because of this, officers have every right to use any and all means appropriate to protect themselves. Most of the people who complain about the police have probably never ridden with an officer, particularly at night, nor do they have a clear idea what actually goes on in the streets. Good officers do want action, meaning they want to be part of what is happening, but they do not go around creating action so they can notch their belts. They face quite enough negative activity on the streets without creating it.

For these kinds of reasons, many veterans today look at their profession as one that is undergoing change that is not necessarily for the best, particularly for the "in-the-trenches" officers. The constant questioning wears on them, makes them feel untrusted, and builds tensions. Their job is challenging enough as it is without having ill-informed people influencing or forcing the reshaping of policies that affect how they do their jobs.

At the time of this writing, the city of Boise has created a new position that is designed to provide a liaison between the community, the city council, and the police department—a police ombudsman. The position is one in which an individual investigates any complaint against the police, then seeks to resolve the problem. This person would also be involved in developing new policies. By its very nature—a complaint office against the police—it will most likely antagonize the corps of officers trying to do their jobs. To even create such a position is an affront to the police department, sending the message that they cannot be trusted as things now are and that someone needs to serve as a spokesperson for the underdog to make sure the police aren't getting away with things. To actually believe that one person, or a small committee working with that person, can realistically be expected to help shape policy for a department of two hundred twenty-five sworn officers based on citizen complaints, borders on magical thinking.

The first person selected for the position, Kristi McKown, gave up her appointment one week after being offered the job. It was publicly disclosed, after her selection was announced as Boise's ombudsman, that she had applied to be a Boise police officer in 1997, then abandoned that pursuit when Mark Stall was killed. The media and city officials seemed to raise their eyebrows at this revelation, and undoubtedly Kristi immediately saw the handwriting on the wall—to be pro-police going in the door was a no-no, and she would have had an uphill battle from day one. Apparently, supposed neutrality or even an anti-police bias would be more acceptable for this particular position, in spite of the fact that the office deals entirely and only with the police and their functions.

Mayor Brent Coles immediately selected another candidate, who was not on the original list, and announced his choice to the city without city council approval. That, too, produced a reaction that caused candidate number two, Richard Mabbutt, to be asked to withdraw his name. Two weeks and two aborted launches of the ombudsman position—not what you would call a good start for the city in respect to trying to corral a police department viewed by some as out of control. A third choice, Pierce Murphy, was just selected as this book is completed.

Can an ombudsman be neutral? Hardly. The person who fills this job will have feelings, pro or con, about police in general. He will desire to fill this role on the basis of what has shaped his attitudes in the past with respect to law enforcement.

Should an ombudsman be pro-police? Yes, for three reasons: (1) The office is already designed to accept complaints *against* the police, which from the outset automatically puts an officer on the defensive. (2) An officer's actions are based on situations that require certain responses. They are the keepers of the law by virtue of their jobs; others are potential law breakers by virtue of being confronted. On that basis, an officer must always be upheld as having done what had to be done unless it is clearly evident that he or she mishandled a situation. (3) This person will apparently help shape future policies; therefore, he *must* have an understanding of the police officer's job in order to be able to make good policy.

In a real sense, the ombudsman position is merely a Band-Aid remedy that in and of itself is inadequate to heal deeper problems. Some people strongly wish to go after the police, thinking that an ombudsman will help clear up a lot of the problems that exist in the community. Nothing could be further from reality. What needs to be gone after is the cancer of wickedness throughout the community that our police are forced to face and deal with daily.

Perhaps another perspective on Boise's fatal situations these last three years will provide some second thoughts as to why they happened. Every killing involved a young male, average age twenty-four. Every incident was a night occurrence. Without exception, there was resistance to the police when the young men were confronted. And without exception, the police were forced to make decisions about their own safety based on the actions of those they confronted. Can we say these officers were out of line? Can we legitimately excuse the behavior of the young men who were approached, as though their actions were petty? Would there have been even one death had each of these individuals simply done what they were told to do by an officer?

Before we so readily bad-mouth the police, we need to think. They have an extremely difficult job, and we, the citizens they serve, should not make it harder by constantly questioning their actions and motives. On the whole, police officers are good people who are doing their best to provide us peace and safety.

As for Chief Larry Paulson—may his tribe increase. He has served the city of Boise with honor and integrity. During his tenure as Chief, he has had to work through some extreme situations. It must be understood that his being Chief had nothing whatsoever to do with the fact that seven young men died on the streets of Boise. Each of those individuals made his own foolish choices when confronted by officers doing their duty.

Chief Paulson has been criticized by biased people, and heard unjustified statements about his character and motives. Through it all he has stood tall and earned the respect of those who work under him and with him. What he needs most from the community he has faithfully served for thirty years is support. His integrity will pay dividends for the city in the long haul. Boise has been blessed to have him occupying the Chief's chair during a time of trouble.

What lies ahead for Boise? Hopefully, long years of citizen and police safety and continued community support. As one former policeman wrote in response to Mark's funeral procession, "When...you think no one supports you, remember the people two to three deep all along State Street all the way from downtown to Glenwood! The community supports you, although the media does not."

All of us—family and community—hope that we will not have any more Mark Stalls dying on our streets.

17

From Here to Eternity

When death strikes a family, the feeling of loss is like a ripping away of what used to be. The one taken can never come back, nor can former things ever again exist as they once did. Death is man's greatest enemy, and the most dreaded. After a loved one is gone, survivors tend to relive in their minds what it must have been like to die. They try putting themselves in the deceased person's place, striving to fathom what the experience of passing into eternity could have been like. By doing this, they relive the death experience over and over in their minds, while their own existence continues unabated. It is a strange phenomenon to dwell on the death experience, yet go on living.

Survivors often cope with the reality of their loved one's death experience for a long time afterwards. No one grieves in precisely the same way as another, and not everyone in a family feels the same intensity of emotion. However, all are forced to accept the harsh reality that death, that great enemy, has claimed the one they loved. Death's separations are permanent.

Among the most grievous things about a death is the final good-bye at a grave—to ultimately have to turn away and leave the casket standing alone, thus creating the final moment of contact with the lifeless body of the one who was so loved. Hereafter, in every regard, the separation is permanent. For those who have suffered loss, this moment is one of the most crushingly helpless in all human experience. For some, the despair of this detachment brings on such an overwhelming sense of loss that the soul feels it is drowning in anguish.

Mark Stall's death oppressed his family and his many friends and acquaintances—they had been dealt a terrible blow. But their loss went beyond themselves and entered the greater Boise community, which had emotionally formed a bond to him over the short period of days between his death and funeral. Many people were despondent over his demise, in spite of never knowing him. Something about his sudden death mesmerized them—they were intrigued about who he was and what he represented; he captivated their affections. What was it like to be at the scene that night? What was it like to take a bullet and in a matter of seconds lose consciousness and move toward death? Family and strangers alike grappled with these questions.

Evidence of how deep this grief was came at the conclusion of the committal service at Dry Creek Cemetery. Hundreds of officers, friends, and family occupied the hillside for this final tribute, and when it was over, their grief exploded. Many openly wept, unable to contain their emotions. They felt helpless about releasing a man they had known and loved, or if they did not personally know him, still held close in heart. This was a very hard time.

One year later, this chapter is being written. An entire calendar year has passed, imbued with the relentless reality that Mark Stall is gone. Every day since September 20, 1997, family members have continuously relived the events of that night which so drastically altered their lives. Everything has changed—joy and happiness have been elusive, difficult to recapture. However, one significant blessing has come out of the ashes of this sorrow—the changes effected in lives and homes across the nation. Officers, their spouses, their children, and others outside law enforcement were issued a wake-up call about the brevity of life and the importance of being prepared for eternity. Mark's sacrifice was a large-scale attention-getter.

God has taken this terrible ordeal and used it to produce good in many people's lives. The family obviously struggled with Mark's loss at the time of his death, and they struggle yet; it is a loss they feel daily. In spite of all the good that has come from Mark's death, there have been times when it was honestly felt that the awful cost of giving up Mark could not justify any number of changed lives, no matter how high the count. Even though phenomenal good came about in the lives of those whose lives were affected, they still did not have to endure the sense of loss borne by those nearest to Mark. Yet, in spite of those occasional feelings, most of this family respectfully yield to God's sovereignty in this incident—accepting that He, for reasons known only to Himself, had eternal purposes to fulfill when He allowed Mark to forfeit his life that morning. They try not to react bitterly at God, or proverbially shake their fists at Him because of what He allowed. Instead, with both sadness and resignation, they realize that He had something very special in mind when He called Mark to his eternal home.

Undoubtedly some will view this thinking as illogical, or even absurd. How could Mark's death be for a greater good when he didn't even reach thirty years of age? How could the creation of widowhood and the stripping of a daddy from two little girls be acceptable? What kind of God designs and permits such awful things?

In the process of trying to cope with these and other questions, it has been helpful to weigh the yearning thoughts of Frank Graeff, who experienced the ravages of sorrow in his own life. He asks about whether the Lord really cares.

Does Jesus care when my heart is pained too deeply for mirth or song;
As the burdens press, and the cares distress, and the way grows weary and long?
Does Jesus care when my way is dark with a nameless dread and fear;
As the daylight fades into deep night shades, does He care enough to be near?
Does Jesus care when I've tried and failed to resist some temptation strong;
When for my deep grief there is no relief, though my tears flow all the night long?
Does Jesus care when I've said "goodbye" to the dearest on earth to me;
And my sad heart aches till it nearly breaks, is it aught to Him? Does He see?

This poet captured the essence of human tragedy and sorrow in his questions. He asks what runs through the mind of every mystified, beleaguered human when the acts of God seem unreasonable and illogical. He then answers his own questions:

> *O yes, He cares, I know He cares; His heart is touched with my grief.*
> *When the days are weary, the long nights dreary, I know my Savior cares.*

So, how does one know God really cares, or that He is not cruelly toying with His creation? Wouldn't it seem reasonable that the omnipotent God would do all in His divine power to preserve and protect His children, rather than remove them? As far as Mark Stall is concerned, it seems logical that God would want to shield and prolong his life so that his family would benefit from his presence for a lifetime. What could be better than that? Apparently, to God, something else was better.

The Stall story and what was reflected about him at his funeral can best be understood in light of what he was in respect to God. He was a sinful man like every other person born into this world. While he was known as a good boy, a respectful teenager, and a responsible young adult, he started life with one significant deficiency—the lack of knowing God in a personal way. However, his parents faithfully instilled the principles of the Bible in their children, and as a result Mark embraced Jesus Christ as his personal Savior at an early age. He gladly accepted Scripture as an important guide to his life.

Over the years of chronological growth, Mark also developed spiritually. Sometimes he grew lax in his spiritual growth, and realized that he needed to renew and strengthen his commitment to God. When he entered law enforcement, he knew he had taken on a vocation that would test his character. He was aware that he would face the ugly side of humanity to such a degree that he would be forced to put his commitment to biblical integrity on trial. Could he honestly do this job and honor God at the same time? He felt he could, and he tried.

It could be done either one of two ways: he could work at being an example of a principled Christian man, or he could still strive to do his job well without making his Christian commitment important to the conduct of his job. He could make it count with his brethren in blue, or he could quietly work without being distinctively known as a Christian cop. It is possible to be a good cop without embracing God, but for him it was not possible to be the right kind of cop without an internal commitment to the God he had come to love and follow. He well knew his flaws, but he was always driven to live, work, and reflect God as integral to his life. Those who knew him knew Mark was a straight arrow.

This being so, why would God remove him, along with the potential positive influence on his brothers in blue, the community, or others his life might have across the years?

Someone recently asked, "Why?" from a different perspective: "Why was Satan allowed to have his way with Mark?" This question seeks to discern why God permitted the devil to make Mark Stall the victim of his dark schemes, and why he fell to evildoers when he was one of God's own. These are reasonable questions. For those who believe in the benevolence of God as well as His omnipotence, the "whys" of such happenings loom in their minds.

A well-known historical happening from very long ago may help explain a tragedy such as this. It involved Satan, better known as the devil according to Scripture, and it is therefore possible that Satan was also involved in Mark's case. The most baffling aspect, however, is that behind all that transpired was the permission of Almighty God.

A familiar Old Testament figure was Job, who is best known for his extreme sufferings. However, prior to the intense heartaches and afflictions that touched him, he had become a very prosperous man. He had a large and loyal family (ten children), many possessions, and a bright and promising future. But unknown to him, things were happening in the heavens that would dramatically change his life on earth. God Himself invited Satan's attention to Job, not once, but twice. It was a baffling invitation on God's part.

"The Lord said to Satan, 'Have you considered My servant Job, that there is none like him on the earth?'" (Job 1:8; 2:3). This was like saying "sic 'em" to a bloodhound. Satan, who is totally evil, said, "Let me have him, and he will end up cursing You to Your face." (Job 1:11; 2:5). Amazingly, God granted Satan permission to touch Job's life—to strip him of his family, his possessions, and his health. The only restriction was that he was not allowed to kill Job, though he apparently had that liberty with Job's children. Satan then proceeded, by several means, to set in motion his heartless and devious plans: marauding bands of men killed Job's servants and stole his possessions; forces of nature such as fire and wind destroyed his family and other holdings; and last of all, he suffered painful and debilitating physical afflictions. In two separate waves of destruction and harm, Satan used his power to strike out at Job.

It might be asked how this ancient biblical account relates to the death of Mark Stall. For one thing, Mark was one of God's children. For another, Satan enjoys the power and ability to enact devastation against mankind, and a person like Mark Stall, a God-fearing police officer, would certainly make an inviting target for harm. Also, Satan wants nothing more than to decimate God's people. Any opportunity that he is allowed will therefore be used to bring evil into the lives of those he hates.

To augment his deliberate wickedness, the devil also holds the ability and means to influence already evil people; he stimulates them to wreak havoc. In this case, on a September night in 1997, he stirred up certain people and generated violence through them. Caught in the centrifugal force of his plan was one of God's people—Mark Stall. Satan intended to destroy and in fact did; but presiding over this violent destruction was God Himself, who allowed Satan to go so far as to take Mark down in death. We can reach no other conclusion: God had special purposes for allowing what seems so illogical, even as He did long ago with Job when He solicited Satan's attention to a significantly righteous man.

Does this assuage the pain of losing Mark Stall? Not in the least. However, it creates the possibility for acceptance in the hearts of those who trust God that, in spite of what is so painful, He remains in control. Satan can and does cause terrible damage and destruction, but he will not and cannot win the war between good and evil. Though God's ways appear mysterious and baffling, He must be trusted to do right because of His perfect standard. Because He is God, He cannot fail or err. He does not purposelessly allow harm to His own, nor does He permit His adversary to touch His children without meaningful reasons. We obviously cannot see or understand the complete meaning of God's actions this side of heaven, but we do know that Satan will be the loser in eternity to come. What is baffling now will then be clear.

To bring the above perspectives into focus in regard to September 20, 1997 allows us to see that Satan intended to destroy a good man's life, and accomplished his purpose. He utilized people with a destructive mindset and arranged a scenario whereby evil purposes would be carried out. But this perspective also requires acceptance of a master plan by God that overrides Satan's evil plan. God possesses the capacity to bring to pass righteous purposes in spite of Satan's destructive actions.

That this is so can be seen in the phenomenal public response to Mark's death, response which went far beyond simple emotional reactions. Enormous spiritual changes were brought to countless homes and individuals.

Some began looking within themselves and realized that they were unprepared to die; they were not in any respect ready to meet God. They began asking what they needed to do to prepare; and subsequently, some took deliberate steps toward being reconciled to the God Mark loved and followed.

By way of example, some months after Mark's death a ranking officer in another police department in Idaho shared that he had not only been affected, but also changed by this tragedy. His wife affirmed that he was not the same man as before. He embraced Christ as his Savior from his sins, then became a faithful part of a nearby church in order to nourish his newfound faith. In another case, a police wife met Cheryl in a mall and embraced her in tears. The woman proceeded to share with the new widow that Mark's sacrifice had actually saved their marriage. She and her husband had been planning to split up the very weekend Mark died; instead, the impact of Mark's death caused them to reconcile with each other and with God. They were now moving on with their lives centered positively in the things that matter most.

Long-time Idaho residents, who have witnessed numerous significant events in Boise and throughout the state of Idaho over the years, testified that they have never seen anything that has had greater impact on the community than Mark's death and funeral. Some likened the spiritual effect to be equal to or even greater than that of the Billy Graham Crusade in Boise years earlier. It has been calculated that Mark's funeral was the largest ever held in Boise, and perhaps in the entire state. Live television coverage extended the impact even further.

Thus, what Satan meant as devastating harm against Mark and his family, God meant for good in the sense that it would accomplish eternal good. No mortal can accurately measure the value of Mark's sacrifice this side of heaven, but perhaps God will reveal His overall purpose in eternity. If so, it will be shown that Mark did not die in vain, though now it seems to have been such a needless death. What cannot be fully known is the extent to which his short life affected countless people across the land because he was an honorable man and loved his God. For that, God must be respectfully honored for bringing about eternal good.

What should this mean to you, the reader? For one thing, it should alert you to give serious consideration to eternal matters in your own life. One of the greatest areas of neglect among most of us is after-death preparations—we too easily view the afterlife as something too distant to think about now. Part of this is because we do not want to think about our mortality, nor do we take seriously enough how critical God considers preparation to be. We wish to deal with death and what comes after it according to our own criteria; therefore, we formulate in our minds what we believe is to come, if anything at all, then go on living based on our own conclusions. But one thing is true for all of us—we yearn for continued life, to continue living beyond this mortal plane. We sense that there must be more to come. The reason is because God has put eternity within us (Ecclesiastes 3:11).

We will each live our short while on earth, then die. What then? None of us can detach ourselves from our mortality; we are inescapably burdened with the inability to beat death. Therefore, we have no choice but to weigh the meaning of our mortality and to realistically consider the eternity before us. Many people forego contemplation of the hereafter by making themselves believe it doesn't really matter—that whatever is meant to be will be, and we will just have to let it come on its own terms. Yet, within each of us is a wondering, a pondering, that is not satisfied with the perspective that death ends it all and we pass into oblivion. We sense that there is more, and in so doing, must inquire as to the nature of what lies ahead. Is it really that important to prepare for the hereafter?

The hereafter, the great beyond, eternity—whatever man wants to call it—is not insignificant according to what God has had to say about it. Eternity exists because God is eternal. He created each of us with the spirit of life, and while man has brought mortality upon himself by the cancer of sin, that spark and spirit of life continues. Mortal death ends physical life here, but it does not end existence. We awaken on the other side of death.

Solomon spoke about this in Ecclesiastes 12. He likened the death experience to the losing of familiar and valuable items which were known to his era: the severing of a silver cord, the breaking of a golden bowl, the shattering of a pitcher at the fountain of water, and the breaking of the wheel which brings up the water at the well-head. Then the dust will return to the earth as it was, and the spirit will return to God who gave it. Man will then have gone to his eternal home (Ecclesiastes 12:5-7).

Does this mean everyone goes back to God after death with the hope and assurance of eternal bliss? No. The sinful soul of man must be prepared to dwell with a holy God. Because man has become unholy and lives in a condition of sinfulness within his soul, he must be reconciled to God so that he and God can dwell together in peace and righteousness. This is why preparation for eternity must take place on earth. Every mortal must prepare to meet God on His terms.

Some will contend that this is mere religion, which may not be acceptable to their point of view. However, religion is not the issue here—God, sin, death, and eternity are the issues. We must leave religion out of the equation and consider the essence of human existence and God's role in it. The Bible is the book that speaks to these things, for if the Bible is not considered valid as God's message to mankind, what can we rely on to satisfactorily help us deal with the issues of life and eternity? The Bible hides nothing; it tells it straight. The Scriptures are God's instructions to those He created about how they are to prepare to come to terms with Him after they have sinned. Since man is eternal, which means he will live beyond this mortal life, God is telling him how eternity is to be prepared for while still on earth.

Mark Stall did this. He aligned himself with God by recognizing his own sinfulness and accepting God's sacrifice for sin, Jesus Christ. He prepared himself for eternity, not knowing how long or short his life on earth would be, and that decision on his part means everything to his family. They rest assured that Mark has inherited eternal life, and are comforted that he has entered his heavenly rest because he was prepared. They have the blessed assurance that he is safe in the arms of Jesus.

Death is the crucial testing point as to how strongly we truly rely on what we believe about hope and eternity. Many in Mark's family rest confidently in this very reliance. They themselves have prepared for eternity, and are comforted that Mark did likewise. They know they have a reunion coming and that the separation will be brief.

So, what about you? What about your preparations? Are you sure about your destiny after this mortal life? The Bible holds the answer to your future. Take it to heart and rest assured that you, too, can have eternal life.

Mark Stall is at home. His family and friends who know the God he once knew only by faith but now knows face to face, are not yet home, but they are on their way. From here to eternity, we abide in hope. May you do likewise.

Tributes to Mark Stall

The death of Mark Stall brought cards, letters, poems, tributes, drawings, and gifts from across the nation. From Maine and Massachusetts in the east, Montana and North Dakota in the north, North and South Carolina in the south, and all the states on the west coast—letters, cards, and heartfelt messages were sent to the Stall family, the police department, or First Security Bank. A retired Los Angeles Police Department Sergeant and a retired West Hollywood, California detective sent comforting messages to Cheryl. Even as these pages are written, a video of Mark's funeral is being circulated among New York State policemen.

Honor upon honor was bestowed upon him posthumously, and his family accepted many awards in his name throughout the year following his death. Some of the significant commendations and praises for his sacrifice are set forth in the Appendix, and some here. These pages share with the reader a sampling of some of the messages from family, friends, colleagues, and strangers. It can by no means include all that has been said and written—that would require another sizeable book. Because of space limitations, many touching notes and messages must be omitted; however, those included are representative of the many heart-warming communications.

From **Louis Freeh**, Director of the Federal Bureau of Investigation: "I was deeply saddened to learn of the death of your husband and want to extend my heartfelt sympathy to you and your children...Your husband's efforts in law enforcement on behalf of the citizens of Boise will not be forgotten...Marilyn and I will keep you in our prayers and ask God to strengthen you in His grace and peace."

From **Lewis Merletti**, Director of the United States Secret Service: "When a member of the law enforcement community loses his life in the line of duty, we all share in the loss. I hope it will be comforting for you to know that the sorrow you feel is not yours alone, but it is being shared by each of us. We will keep you and your children, Jonelle and Julia, in our thoughts and prayers."

From Idaho Governor **Philip Batt:** "This was a terrible tragedy, the depths of which have been felt by citizens across our great state...Mark was a fine, upstanding young man—devoted to you, his children and family, and dedicated to his job. As a police officer he protected and served Idahoans selflessly, and as an individual, he touched the lives of so many."

From U. S. Senator **Larry Craig:** "Suzanne and I, on behalf of my staff, wish to express our sincere condolences to you and your family in this difficult time. Clearly, Mark was a human being of the highest caliber, who chose and excelled in the noblest of professions—serving his fellow man. We should seek solace in the understanding that each of us fills a role in the Lord's grand plan. Mark's place is now at His side."

From U.S. Congressman **Mike Crapo:** "My wife, Susan, and I were deeply saddened to hear of the recent loss of your husband, Mark...The service he performed in the line of duty for his community is commendable. I know many others share your sorrow and recognize the sacrifice your family has made."

From the Idaho Speaker of the House of Representatives **Michael Simpson:** "It is with a heavy heart that I wish to offer my condolences to you and your family at this very sad time. I know that you moved to this community because it seemed a safe haven in which to raise your children. Words cannot express how sorry we are to have let you down. Please know that you are in the thoughts and prayers of a grateful city."

From Idaho Attorney General **Alan Lance:** "We are all at a loss as to why this has happened. We must trust that our faith in God and our country will help us through this very difficult time. Mark's generosity and his commitment to the City of Boise will be missed by all."

Some of the most moving messages came from families who have also suffered the loss of a police officer in the line of duty. The parents of Timothy Blaine Howe shared how their son died at the hands of a drug dealer on Good Friday, April 14, 1995. He was only thirty-four years of age and was engaged to be married six weeks later. They wrote, "The pain is still very vivid even today. We don't know if it will ever cease."

Kathleen Steed of Caldwell, Idaho wrote Cheryl to share that she, too, is the widow of a slain police officer. She was but twenty-six and her husband Richard a month short of his thirtieth birthday, when he died in San Clemente, California nineteen years ago. She stated, "I still have deep feelings every time an officer is lost."

Oregon State Trooper Bill Lyons lost his son in the line of duty only two weeks before Mark's death. His son was also a State Trooper. He wrote, "You are probably feeling this whole situation is so unfair, and you're right...it's not fair. It's not fair that good, responsible police officers are taken from their families. Please know we are grieving with you, just like our own son. They didn't know each other either, but they were brother officers."

A most touching letter came from Vicki Jeffries, a young Oregon widow whose husband died in the line of duty in Portland two months before Mark. He was shot to death attempting to arrest a man who had just shot a seven-year old boy. Vicki movingly wrote, "When I learned of your husband's death, I grieved at the thought of another person subjected to the indescribable pain of losing a beloved spouse. I adored my dear Tom. We had just celebrated our second anniversary and were expecting our first baby to be born in ten weeks when Tom was killed. The baby is now due in one week, and I am hoping to take some comfort in his arrival. I hope your children will provide some solace to you. I truly wish you every last ounce of strength I have. I pray no one would have to experience how impossibly painful a loss such as ours is. I am so very sorry." Cheryl and some of the family met Vicki in Alexandria, Virginia in May 1998 when all were in attendance for the National Police Week. She delivered a healthy baby, but her life has been ripped to pieces.

One of the most chilling messages was found among the signatures on a thoughtful card from the Payette County Sheriff's Office in Payette, Idaho. It was a hand-written note from Linda Huff, who would lay down her own life nine months later in June 1998. Prior to serving as an Idaho State Trooper, she served as a deputy in the Payette County Sheriff's Department. The largest and longest of the forty-five signatures and notes on the card to Cheryl and her girls read, "Deputy Linda Huff. He will guide you in your time of need!

God Bless You," followed by a smiley face. Ironically, Linda's state badge number was the same as Mark's Ada County badge number—512.

One of the most tender letters was written by Tara Parker, the daughter of Mark's oldest sister, Linda. Tara's daddy died when she was only four years old. Now fifteen, she wrote Mark a letter the day before his funeral. "Dear Uncle Mark: Though I write this physical letter, you see and read it spiritually. Remembering way back to your wedding, I would not let you marry because I thought that it would take you away from me forever. You helped raise me; you were my father for those years after. Physically I know you are not on earth, but you are here, and you won't leave. Thank you, Lord, now all we need to do is count down the days till we go and be with You. I can't believe that you are talking to my dad right now. I'm so jealous. You helped teach me right from wrong. And I want you to know that your girls are in my hands and I will not let anything happen to them that you or God wouldn't approve. I love you. Your niece, Tara. P.S. Say hi to my daddy. Thank you."

The Mountain View, California Police Chief, Mike Maehler, and his wife Gail, also sent special greetings to Cheryl. Mark was born in Mountain View, which gives added significance to their thoughtful card. Also, one of Mark's boyhood friends, Dave Spiller, is an officer in the Mountain View Police Department. Dave served as one of Mark's pallbearers.

Dave wrote a moving tribute to Mark in his department's newsletter two weeks after Mark's death. "I went to Boise to say goodbye to my friend, and found myself overwhelmed with the effect he had on that community. I stood at the scene where the darkness of that senseless altercation took Mark's life, and I discovered hundreds of plants, flowers, cards and candles left by community members mourning Mark's death. Everything that I had witnessed during my stay in Idaho was truly a tribute to a great man. After the memorial service, I drove Mark's family in the procession of police vehicles. As we traveled the streets of Boise I was astonished to see literally thousands upon thousands of people lining the streets to pay tribute to Officer Mark Stall. Schoolchildren wore blue ribbons to honor his passing, men and women held signs with their eyes full of tears. Again it truly made me see just how many lives my friend had touched. I was saddened to see what a role model and hero this city has lost.

"As I carried my friend to his grave, then sat with his wife and mother, I reflected on my childhood growing up with Mark and what a positive influence he had on me. Mark was a very devout man of God. A religious man with an ever-increasing faith, Mark had the highest morals and values stronger than I'd ever seen. I was happy to have known Mark, to have been a part of this man's life, and I am a better person for knowing him."

Deputy Margaret Mountan of the Los Angeles Sheriff's Office wrote, "I worked with Mark and loved it! He was a great deputy, but more importantly, he was a great man. When I picture him, I see him smiling. I can't picture him not smiling!"

Deputy James Williams of the Los Angeles Sheriff's Office wrote about serving with Mark in 1990 as Deputy/Drill Instructors for what was called the Regimented Inmate Diversion Program (RID Program) at Pitchess Honor Ranch outside Los Angeles. This was a test program which was basically a prison boot camp.

Williams wrote about rolling his truck in 1991 on the way home from one of his long shifts. He was taken to a hospital, where he was treated for his injuries and then released. Mark had retrieved his gear from the wreckage and was there to take him home from the hospital. He wrote, "During our ride to my place, he provided me with comforting conversation and support. I don't think I ever told him how much I really appreciated his help that night. So, now I tell you."

Another young friend to the Stall family wrote: "Dear Ray and Nancy: I do not know how you feel. I cannot even imagine the pain of losing a son so suddenly. Of all the children you have had, Mark was the one I knew the most. I have nothing but pleasant memories of this man. I knew him as a role model, a godly man, and a friend. I am sure he spurred his fellow officers on to do the correct thing. My focus is on nothing but Jesus because of Mark and you both."

A special friend to Mark was David Sandoval, a young Hispanic man he befriended in Los Angeles in the late 1980's. David worked with and for Mark at the Master's College in painting and maintenance, and still is employed at the College. David came to Boise the Christmas before Mark's death to spend time with the Stall family. It snowed while he was there, and he was thrilled beyond words to see the snow falling. He had Jonelle and Julia bury him in the white stuff until only his face could be seen. David came to Boise because he loved Mark very dearly and wanted to see his friend again after several years.

When David came to Boise for Mark's funeral nine months later, he was in total shock. He was in another world of pain and sorrow. He wrote a note to Mark the day before the funeral: "Mark, you will be on my heart for the rest of my life! God bless you. Your amigo del alma." On the first anniversary of Mark's death, David from Los Angeles arranged for a beautiful bouquet to be sent to remember his special friend. He thanked Mark for introducing him to Jesus Christ and for being his friend.

Several communications came from Pennsylvania. One was from a man whose father served as a Pennsylvania State Policeman for thirty years. At least three other cards and letters came from the area where the Brodrick family lives. The first came from a State Trooper from Indiana, Pennsylvania who wrote, "We are deeply sorry about Mark's death. Your family is in our prayers and thoughts. You have the sympathy and support of my fellow brothers and sisters here in Pennsylvania." Another came with a donation and note from the Borough of Indiana Police Department. "The money is presented out of respect for a fellow officer and as a token memorial to a fallen comrade." The last came from a group of individuals who were quite direct about what had happened: "Dear Mrs. Stall: Several of us feel very bad back here in Indiana County, PA about what happened, and feel very bad that the two that murdered your husband, Officer Mark Stall, came from our small community. Please accept our deepest sympathy. We are very sorry."

Several families who have lost family members to violent crimes also wrote. One lady shared, "Words cannot express the pain I feel for your loss. I am the daughter of a retired police officer. I am also the widow of an ordinary citizen who was shot and killed, leaving me to raise our five children by myself. They were two, five, six, eight, and ten at the time my husband was murdered eighteen years ago. God has brought us through, and He is there for you, too."

Another family deeply affected by a violent crime wrote, "Having attended Mark's funeral yesterday, we were struck with the remarkable courage and unyielding faith that you and your family have demonstrated. We are deeply saddened by the tragic death of Mark and realize that your burden is heavy. We are renewed, however, with the inspiring words of so many and the outpouring of love and support. We too are victims of violent crime—a senseless act perpetrated by two men has left our family devastated for the rest of our natural lives. Although our hearts are broken, we must go forward to love and serve the Lord and carry out His plan for each of us."

A newer friend to Mark wrote Cheryl, "I was introduced to Mark a few months ago by a mutual friend. I had gone on a ride-along with Mark and was very impressed with him. He was a true professional and was very candid with me in his expression of how much he loved you and the girls. I also want you to know that at my church...the guest preacher had read of Mark's story in the paper...(he) used the incident in his message with great impact. Four people accepted Jesus as their personal Savior. I believe Mark's story was instrumental in those decisions, and will be in others to come."

In December 1997, Linda Puryear of Nampa, Idaho was so touched by Cheryl's loss that she had six T-shirts made showing support for Idaho Law Enforcement and dedicated to Mark Stall. Soon she found that family and friends also wanted a shirt, and the idea was born to raise money for Cheryl and her daughters. She at first aimed for $100, but that amount was quickly surpassed. In a matter of weeks she raised over $1200, and when she finally phased out, she had raised over $1500 for Cheryl and the girls! Most shirts went to Idahoans, but she also sold shirts to people in Virginia, Mississippi, Alabama, Texas, Oregon, and Alaska. Later, she met Cheryl for the first time and presented her with a check. In an earlier letter to Cheryl, Linda wrote, "I would like to say that I truly admire your strength and faith during this time of your life. You are an inspiration."

One young woman, who was interviewed during Mark's funeral procession, spoke of how she had once been stopped by Mark. She was going through a hard time in her life and had little appreciation for the police. Mark found that she had no automobile insurance, and patiently listened as she told him why not. He finally told her she couldn't afford insurance and the ticket both, so he might "lose her ticket" if she would go and do the right thing about her insurance. With much emotion, she shared how much that had meant to her, and how it had helped restore her faith in the police.

A special letter along with a $1000 donation to the Stall Memorial Trust came from the Idaho Emergency Physicians. They wrote, "Please accept this contribution...in recognition of the dedication and example of Mark Stall as a husband, father, citizen, and policeman...Your strength and faith during this most difficult time is an inspiration to the entire community. May God continue to bless and comfort you."

A woman wrote Cheryl about a terrible scene she had witnessed two years earlier, in which a woman was screaming and a man supposedly had a gun. The woman used "horrible, horrible language," she wrote, and with her were two or three small children, crying and very afraid. The police were called, and arrived on the scene shortly. The lady shared that one officer was with the screaming woman, another with the man, and "there with his arms around the children was your Mark, speaking to them with compassion on his face. I was so thankful for your husband that day!"

A kind letter came to Cheryl from a Boise man she had never met. He wrote: "Mark became a prevalent part of my life many months past. I didn't know him well, but unknown to him, I would remember him—and you (and his family) in my prayers EVERY day. Each time an incident would occur, I'd call the Boise Police and ask, 'Was Mark involved?' This time, though, for reasons unknown to me, I didn't. I was totally unaware that it was my friend Mark who had been shot until I was watching the news. At first I was stunned, then I broke down—I haven't cried so much in years! I've been a zombie ever since...I don't know if he ever mentioned to you that some guy would buy him Kit-Kat candy. I'm that guy!!!..."

The Dispatch personnel of the city and county wrote, "We miss Mark more than words can express. Not only have we lost a co-worker, we have lost our friend." A police wife shared, "I couldn't help but rejoice over how strong your faith is and what witness you, Mark, and your family have been to so many. My husband, too, is a police officer, and feels your pain deeply. Your husband, father, son, and brother was a man deserving of honor and respect. I praise God for him and rejoice he is in a better place." A woman in Records for the county and city said, "It is a pleasure to assist officers who are kind and respectful of our job, and Mark truly was...remember how blessed you were to have met such a wonderful man and shared such wonderful years with him...Mark will be missed very much!" Another lady from Records wrote, "Mark was always uplifting to us when he came into Records."

One brother officer wrote, "Mark: Thank you so much for blessing us all with your short visit here on earth. There will be a true void in our lives until we meet again in heaven. We love you, Mark. Goodbye, beloved friend." Another high-ranking officer wrote

Cheryl, "All our thoughts are with you. I wish it could have been me instead."

During the weeks around Christmas 1997, a card was taped to Mark's cross at his grave with a poem from a brother officer. It read, "Then spoke brave Horatius, the Captain of the gate. `To every man upon this earth death cometh soon or late. And how can man die better than facing fearful odds? For the ashes of his fathers and the temple of his God.' Merry Christmas, Bro. We miss you..."

A thoughtful little card was found after Mark's funeral addressed to Officer Mark Stall c/o God in Heaven. "Dear Officer Stall: I've spent some time thinking about what to say, but words can't do justice to what you've given me and the people of this community. In the end all I can say is thank you for giving your life to protect us. You will never be forgotten."

Many others were written. One said, "We thank God for Mark! We thank Mark for reminding us of God!" Another wrote, "I will miss you. You may not know it, but you made a big change in my life. And I will forever remember you. Thank you."

One unsigned card read, "Officer Stall: Three weeks ago, you came into our lives. You did two things: you gave my daughter courage to do the right thing, and you left us with much hope! You are our hero."

Another stated, "Thank you, Officer Stall! You served us and protected us from evil...God bless you!!!" A couple left this kind expression, "We've always *quietly* honored our police force by simply obeying the law, being courteous to strangers, and standing ready to help those in need, like you and your colleagues. Your sacrifice, Mark, makes us feel that perhaps we need to do more...To you and your fellow peace officers: thanks always for your love."

A note that appeared to be written by a child said, "In memory of Mark Stall. We were touched by his kindness when he stopped to help us get gas for are car. We will never for get his kindness."

And from two friends: "We'll miss you Mark. And we'll see you again someday, in peace. Thank you, Mark, for letting me remember God again! I will live tomorrow and each day to follow in His glory."

An intriguing letter addressed to Mark delivered a powerful message: "Dear Mark Stall: You have been a big inspiration to me. Our community misses you deeply. You know, you have set an example to all of us in many different ways...I used to have the immature, brainless, hate-filled view of police officers and law enforcement. Due to growing up and being accountable, I am living a much more fulfilling life without having to blame others for society's problems and mine. It's time to take a stand. Now, because of you and others like you, I will get involved. You, Mark Stall, have given me reason to stand up and fight for what I believe...People like you, Mark, are greatly needed. Your life, and your death, were greatly honored and needed...I pray for your family, your children and wife especially, that they move on and prosper and know that Mark Stall was a teacher with many lessons; that they stay strong for each other; that your daughters will grow up and have the same strength and courage and faith as you. You made a difference, Mark Stall. Love—25 yr. old ex-con."

It is fitting that tributes include poems written about and to Mark, as they reflect the depth of feeling from the person writing. One lady, a bus driver for the Meridian School District, wrote, "The day of Mark's funeral, I watched and wept between my bus runs...When I am deeply moved, I write a poem. While I drove my bus, this poem came to me."

An officer has fallen! Our hearts cry out in grief.
He gave his life in service. His life was all too brief.
An officer has fallen! His message rings so clear.
Give all you have to others, but do not live in fear.
An officer has fallen! He gave his very best.
He gave that we might live in peace. He passed the greatest test.
An officer has risen! He's climbed to greater height.
And sits among the chosen to share eternal light.

Another unknown individual wrote these thoughtful words:

I never knew you in life
But now after your tragic death,
I am thankful.
Thankful for your dedication
Thankful for your will to serve others
Thankful that you followed the will of God.
Thankful you were able to say goodbye to your family.
I pray now that this city continues to show support.
Support for your wife

Support for your daughters too young to be fatherless
Support for the Boise Police Department
Support for your entire family.
The hearts of many have gone out.
May these same hearts allow your wife and daughters time to grieve.
I plead to Boise to let them have time.
Grieve
Grieve for your soulmate,
Grieve for your friend,
Grieve for your father,
Grief `til the end.
Thank you, Lord Jesus, for Mark,
A true follower of God.

One of the teens in Mark's church, Matt Basinger, age sixteen, had the opportunity to work with Mark on some of his paint and deck jobs. An outstanding young man, Matt felt compelled to write a tribute to Mark. In so doing, he said, "Writing this poem about Mark was extremely difficult...no words can really express what a special person he was and all he taught me. As countless others have said, there was no question about Mark's faith, and I have found great comfort in this. I know the memories I have, and things I learned from him will always remain intensely alive in me until we see each other again."

The silent shock came early morning,
We were left alone without a warning.
The call we got, the news we heard;
My heart, first broken, was then assured.
At first I thought we'd all been cheated,
But now I find we weren't mistreated.
We seem to view this as a loss,
But in doing so, forget the cross.
For I believe God had a plan
Or reason why He took this man.
This man I try to show to you,
This man whose love for God was true.
He loved to work; he loved to lead.
It seemed that serving was his need.
He had a special zest for life,

Two little children and a wife.
He answered all the midnight calls
And still had time to paint the walls.
He completed many a task and deed
That no one else could, but did need.
I worked two summers by his side—
More than my friend, he was my guide.
I found him all I wished to be:
True to God, his friends, and family.
He believed in truth and lived that way.
Is that why he's not here today?
For now we must remain apart
Though he is with me in my heart.
Someday yet I'll see Mark's face
Redeemed in Heaven by God's grace.

A co-worker wrote a note to a friend of Mark and Cheryl, "Your faith in God is truly an inspiration to me...I have jotted down the words to a song that seemed to me to fit Mark (pretentious I know, considering I didn't know him very well). I know that it's not exactly a religious song, but I thought it was beautiful and wanted to share it with you."

Once in a while, someone comes along
That one in a million heart, so pure and so strong
Once in a while, someone has the eyes
That one in a million look, that never tells lies
They can get you on your feet to walk that extra mile
And we only get them every once in a while.
That's why we call them heroes
That's why we know their names
And once you've heard their stories
You're never quite the same.
That's why we call them heroes
And the best thing they ever do
Is point to the best in us all
And say, if I can, you can too.
Once in a while, I still hear his voice
That one in a million sound, like two laughing boys

He would hate it if we cried, that never was his style
But, oh, we still miss him, every once in a while.
Oh, how I miss him, every once in a while.

Matt and Kim Buie, who both worked as dispatchers when Mark died, had a special bond with Mark and Cheryl. Kim wrote her co-workers a lengthy letter the day of Mark's death, in which she shared her heart about Mark: "What has taken place tonight is a horrible tragedy. Matt and I were close friends with Mark and his family; we shared a common bond, and that bond was Jesus Christ. It began with an acquaintance at work, and through mutual friends developed into a friendship. We were concert buddies. In the past year we went to three different concerts together. We always went to dinner beforehand and to Mark and Cheryl's afterwards for good conversation and Schwan's ice cream. In fact, we were looking forward to this coming Tuesday night when we would be getting together again for the same fellowship. But that was not to be. Matt and I loved to be around Mark and Cheryl and their two daughters. They were such an encouragement to us in our faith, and an example of the kind of parents we want to be whenever the Lord blesses us with children." Kim then ended with: "I will just leave you with the lyrics of one of the songs we would have heard on Tuesday night by artist Jaci Valasquez.

You've got to live every moment,
As though it was your last
Before the thief of always
Steals tomorrow from your grasp.
Before the chance to know His love
Has somehow passed you by.
Let your heart reach out
Right here, right now
For the Lord to touch your life

Awards, Honors, and Commendations

The name Mark Stall became synonymous with honors and commendations in the months following his death. The first to come was from the United States Marshal of Pittsburgh, Pennsylvania. A beautiful plaque in memory of Mark was sent to Cheryl, along with the well-known Law Enforcement poem, "A PART OF AMERICA DIED."

Someone killed a policeman today,
And a part of America died...
A piece of our country he swore to protect
Will be buried with him at his side.
The beat that he walked was a battlefield, too,
Just as if he had gone off to war;
Though the flag of our nation won't fly at half-mast,
To his name they will add a gold star.
The suspect that shot him will stand up in court,
With counsel demanding his rights,
While a young widowed mother must work for her kids,
And spend many lonely nights.
Yes, somebody killed a policeman today,
Maybe in your town or mine.
While we slept in comfort behind our locked doors
A cop put his life on the line.
Now his ghost walks the beat on a dark city street
And he stands at each new rookie's side;
He answered the call, of himself gave his all,
And a part of America died.

The American Police Hall of Fame Medal of Honor Award was issued September 24, 1997—the day of Mark's funeral.

The City of Boise selected Mark as Police Officer of the Year 1997 and presented that award to Cheryl at the Mayor's Christmas Party in December 1997 at City Hall.

The Boise Police Department also selected Mark for its annual award for Officer of the Year. His plaque read:

> BOISE POLICE DEPARTMENT
> *Police Officer of the Year*
> *Is hereby awarded to*
> OFFICER MARK STALL
> *for his courage, professionalism, and dedication to duty. In many ways, Mark set the standard of performance for all officers to follow, selflessly giving of himself for the benefit of others. On September 20, 1997, Mark gave his life bravely trying to protect the citizens of Boise through his service, and for the honor that his memory continues to bring, we award him the Boise Police Officer of the Year for 1997.*

The Eagles donated $1000 for the prevention of child abuse in Mark's memory. The plaque presented says, "He was a man of strong conviction who loved God, his community, his family, and gave his all to protect and defend them. We thank you, Mark."

In May 1998, the Idaho Peace Officers' Memorial was dedicated in Meridian, Idaho with the names of forty-nine officers who have lost their lives in the line of duty in Idaho law enforcement history. Mark's name was the last on the wall, but unfortunately did not remain so for long. Linda Huff, the first female officer in Idaho's history to lose her life in the line of duty, will have her name added for 1998. Because of Mark's death in 1997, he was honored at the dedication. His grandfather, Philip Clucas, accepted the honor on behalf of the family.

> MEDAL OF HONOR AWARD
> *Presented in Memory of*
> OFFICER MARK STALL
> *who, in the performance of his duties, gave his life to protect life and property. We honor his memory and the supreme sacrifice he made.*
>
> ~~~~~
>
> *This award is public recognition of the honor in*

which we will forever hold his name by placing
his name on the
Idaho Peace Officer's Memorial
so that his sacrifice and his dedication to
humanity and justice will always be remembered.
May 15, 1998

In early June 1998, the Idaho Special Olympics honored Mark on shirts and by public recognition. Ray and Nancy Stall, Cheryl Stall and her girls, and Arnold and Kay Rubey all participated in the opening ceremonies at Boise State University.

The Idaho Department of Law Enforcement and the Idaho Criminal Justice Association presented their LIFE SAVING AWARD to Mark, "...for your courage and willingness to sacrifice your own life for the lives of your fellow officers. Given on this 10th day of June 1998."

Numerous other awards have been designated in Mark's name, and honors have been bestowed upon him richly. The Boise Police Department retired his locker, #141, and placed on it a permanent oak door with Mark's portrait, as a constant memorial to officers who every day pass that locker. A flagpole and its flag which flew over the U.S. Capitol Building on July 4, 1998, have been donated and erected at the Criminal Investigations Department in Boise, where a plaque will also be placed in his memory.

Boise Mayor Brent Coles announced that the City Council of Boise will name a future park after Mark. That location will be the Hobble Creek Community Park in West Boise. It will include the Mark Stall Memorial Plaza and a playground. A second memorial will be built along the greenbelt in East Boise in the near future..

As the end of the twentieth century nears and we begin the twenty-first, little can be known of what lies ahead. For the Stall family, it is certain that their loss will be felt through the entirety of their lifetimes. Lives go on, and life itself demands that we face the future. All the honors, commendations, plaques, and expressions of support are, in a certain sense, reminders of the terrible losses incurred with the death of Mark Stall. The honors are gratefully accepted, and Mark's memory is rightly perpetuated, but most of all it is wished that no more names go on the wall in Meridian, Idaho or in Washington, D.C. Sadly, however, we know that is not to be.

Epilogue

On the first anniversary of Mark's death, September 20, 1998, the Boise Police Department held a non-advertised candlelight vigil at Mark's gravesite in Dry Creek Cemetery. As twilight passed into darkness, Cheryl Stall-Chamberlain and Jonelle and Julia Stall lit their candles to begin passing the flame through the entire audience of officers, wives, and family of Mark Stall. Chief Larry Paulson shared remarks, as did Ray Stall and Arnold Rubey. Bob King, of the downtown Stinker station that Mark frequented, also paid tribute to how much Mark meant to him. This particular gathering was another stirring experience that reopened the pain of this sad ordeal, yet in another way helped heal some of the deep emotional wounds created by that awful happening a year earlier.

Also heard for the first time was a moving musical tribute to Mark, written by Donna Wells, then of Notus, Idaho. After hearing Arnold Rubey tell the story of Mark's death several weeks earlier, she felt compelled to write the account of his death and funeral with captivating words and music. No one remained unmoved by the sounds and message of her prose.

He readied for work in his usual way,
Taking some time with his daughters to play.
Then with his uniform on, and his gun by his side,
He and his partner went for — his last ride.
Dispatch came on the radio — a call for assistance had been made.
So they turned their car toward the scene,
And went to give their brothers some aid.
TRUE BROTHER IN BLUE, taking a stand,
Always willing to give each other a hand.

TRUE BROTHERS IN BLUE, fighting for right —
Willing to risk their lives, every day and night.
Once on the scene with others answering the call,
It looked like they wouldn't be needed after all.
But on the way to the car the firing did start.
Above the vest the bullet hit, like a fiery dart.
His partner watched as he fell to the ground
And rushed unprotected to his side.
But this wounded brother bravely shot once more
Protecting his partner — even as he died.
FALLEN BROTHER IN BLUE — taking a stand,
While stopping to give his brothers a hand.
FALLEN BROTHER IN BLUE, fighting for right —
Willing to give his life one dark night.
At the memorial service his life was recalled,
As one who served his city and God with his all.
For he had trusted in the work Of Christ on Calvary —
Who had given His life So all who trust Him could be free.
And because of His acceptance Of God's precious Gift of Love,
We can be sure he now resides with his Heavenly Father above.
FALLEN BROTHER IN BLUE, you didn't die in vain.
Through life and death you showed your trust in Jesus' Holy Name.
FALLEN BROTHER IN BLUE, a hero for all to see:
Through life and death you showed the way — to Calvary.
Through life and death you showed the way — to Calvary.
(used by permission)

Many at the vigil were seeing Mark's headstone for the first time. It is a majestic, six-foot-tall stone, beautifully carved by its makers. At the top in multiple colors is the police star, and below the star is Mark's profile in his police uniform, as seen in his portrait at the funeral. The lower part of the stone contains the essence of the sentiments Cheryl and the girls wrote to Mark on his Father's Day card three months before his death. The nostalgic thoughts contained in that message were so suitable and appropriate to Mark's life that they were adapted as prose for the marker. Finally, at the very bottom of the massive stone, are two brass plaques—one from Ray and Nancy Stall to their son, and the other from Mark's brother and sisters.

The headstone reads as follows:
MARK ARLIN STALL
November 17, 1967
September 20, 1997
A hero to us — your wife, daughters, and family
Adored, prayed for, sung about, longed for
Your daughters hold you up high
Your wife was blessed to have you as her loving husband
You were a father and husband who loved us more than life itself
Yes, you are our hero — today, tomorrow, and forever
For being part of our lives, and for being who you were
Was God's gift to us for earth's short while and for eternity
We will love you always

Ray and Nancy Stall's message to their son reads as follows:
We thank GOD for the joy you brought.
You gave honor and became honored.
You showed respect and became respected.
You loved and we loved you.
MOM AND DAD

The plaque from Mark's brother and sisters reads:
A part of Boise has died, an officer has lost
his life, and our youngest brother, Mark,
full of life and compassion, is now a
missing part of the family left behind.
Our memories of you will live forever in
our hearts.
Your loving brother and sisters,
MATT, LINDA & LOUISE

Dry Creek Cemetery also has memorial benches placed throughout the cemetery, and Cheryl felt that placing one near Mark's grave would be fitting. She had inscribed on the front:
FOR MARK STALL — the best daddy in the world
LOVE ALWAYS Cheryl, Jonelle and Julia

Ray and Nancy Stall, along with Arnold and Kay Rubey, also had a memorial bench placed in Mark's memory at the Idaho Peace Officers' Memorial in Meridian, Idaho.

In memory of Mark Stall
You were a good son. You finished the course with honor, courage,
and faith. We will see you soon.
RAY AND NANCY STALL
ARNOLD AND KAY RUBEY

When November 17, 1998 arrived, it was the date of what would have been Mark's thirty-first birthday. It was a hard day for Cheryl, though it had been fourteen months since Mark's passing. She once again decided that she and the girls would take balloons to the grave, only this time they would all be alike, and each would write a message on a card which would be attached to her balloon and released into the sky. As Cheryl wrote the cards out for each of them while sitting in their Suburban, she sobbed. The pain was still great. Her message to her husband, and their messages to their daddy, were recorded for the sake of remembrance.

Jonelle's note read:

"Dear Daddy: I love you with all of my heart. You were the greatest daddy in the whole world—and a very brave and strong man. You honored our God who we love. Remember your two daughters who love you the most. Love, Your Jonelle (age 7)."

Julia's note read:

"Dear Daddy: I love you with all of my heart. I miss you very much. Thank you for being my best daddy in the whole world. I also love my new daddy God gave me. I can't and will never stop loving you. I also love all my new sisters God gave me. I will never stop loving mommy. Love you. Julia Rae (age 4)."

Cheryl wrote to her missing husband:

"It's your birthday again. You would be 31 this year. We all miss you, but know you're in a much better place. God has been so good to us and blessed us with so much since He took you home. I am so thankful that you were the man of honor and integrity that you were. Thank you for being a wonderful husband and father. You will be remembered ALWAYS! Love, Cheryl."

Cheryl asked her parents to join them for this visit to the cemetery. It was a gloomy afternoon, which mirrored their downcast mood. They stood before Mark's grave for a few moments, then one at a time released their balloons. The gentle breeze carried each balloon and its message high into the sky until they were gone from sight. They floated gracefully upward as though being drawn into the heavens. It was the conclusion to another melancholy day with special meaning.

As the march of time continues, the pain of this experience will hopefully lessen in every affected person's life; yet there is a sense in which the bitterness of this loss must never go away. There must always be a reminder of the depth of pain created by a situation of this nature. The family of Mark Stall can never fully recover from his death, but they will learn to live beyond it. What they cling to that makes such a difference is hope. They know a reunion awaits them in the place where every tear will be wiped away from their eyes, and where there will be no more death, sorrow, crying, or pain (Revelation 21:4). For this they longingly yearn.

Yes, Mark, we will see you again before long.

Appendices

Appendix 1

MAYOR: OFFICER STALL BELIEVED HE COULD MAKE A DIFFERENCE

(Boise Mayor Brent Coles's address to the city
Sunday night, September 21, 1997)

Thank you for spending a few minutes with me tonight. I want to thank our local media for giving me this chance to speak with you.

Our sense of all that we hold sacred within our hearts about the identity of our city has been shaken by the cutting down of Boise Police Officer Mark Stall.

He was shot and killed while serving his community—believing he could make a difference, believing he could keep you safe at night to rest and then wake to a city full of opportunities for raising your family and living your dreams.

It is almost incomprehensible to me that we had someone driving around our community at one o'clock in the morning with a loaded semi-automatic, who used that gun to shoot and kill a police officer. And a family loses a father, a husband, a brother, and a son. My heart aches for that family and their loss.

To the Stall family—when I visited with you last night, I sensed your love and respect for Mark and all that he has done for our community and your family. I sensed your strength, your faith, and your courage in the face of tragedy.

I felt the sweet spirit of family unity from Mark's family and, Cheryl, from your family, as you have come together. Please accept the sympathy and love that the people of Boise will continue to share with you in the difficult weeks ahead.

To Officer Ron Winegar and your family—we are likewise grateful for your strength and your commitment to preserving peace in our community. We are sorry about the injuries you have suffered and pray for a full and speedy recovery.

To the officers that were involved in the firefight on Saturday morning—I know you did all you could do to avoid this tragedy. We as a community are grateful for your courage, your training, and your commitment to our safety.

We know it may take weeks, months, and even years for you to overcome the feelings you have had about that night. But we know you did all you could do to protect and save the lives of your fellow officers, as you put yourselves in harm's way for the sake of our community.

To the community—I want you to understand that our police officers are dedicated to protecting and serving you and your families. Our officers, like the two who were shot Saturday morning, have families. They have dreams. They have hopes. No, they are not perfect, but they are willing to put their lives on the line for us every day and night. Let's not do anything that would jeopardize their ability to fulfill their responsibilities. Our responsibility is to support them while they protect us.

Think back to this spring, when a little girl was kidnapped from her West Boise home. Two important things happened. One—the officers performed superbly, above and beyond the call of duty. And two—the community supported the officers by calling in with information. Thanks to a phone call from a watchful neighbor, officers identified the suspect vehicle and they recovered her uninjured. The point is that we all must work together to keep our community safe.

Now I must ask that, as a community, we set aside this Wednesday to remember Officer Mark Stall. At the request of his family, I invite each of you to bring your families to the Pavilion for the funeral at ten a.m. on Wednesday.

City Hall will be closed so city employees can attend the funeral, and I am asking each business and government agency in Boise to do the same. I ask you to lower your flags to half-staff and to find some way in your workplace Wednesday to honor the memory of Mark Stall.

Tonight I also ask you, as your mayor, to take a few minutes and sit down with your families. Talk about the values you hold dear.

Talk about the people you care for. Talk about your dreams and about the reasons why you live in Boise, Idaho.

Then, as parents and young people, I want you to ask yourselves what your personal response has been when a police officer pulled you over. If you have been cited for something, have you blamed the police officer?

Have you told your kids that it is the officer's fault that you got caught, or did you accept responsibility for your actions and acknowledge that you had broken the law?

Have you tried to shift the blame for your actions, or have you reminded your kids that police officers play an important role in our community and deserve our respect and support?

In every instance where police have been involved in a shooting in the past two years, the bottom line has been that the individuals involved refused to follow the direction of a police officer. The common denominator in each of these cases has been a lack of respect. I suggest to you that none of these incidents would have occurred if individuals had simply followed the officer's directions.

I, like many of you, have wondered aloud to myself and my family why these shootings are happening in Boise. Who can deny that the reason is not that, in every instance, if an officer's command had been obeyed, no death would have occurred? Many ask why the command wasn't obeyed. This answer is much more complex and may be different in each case, but each case has led to the tragic loss of life.

Saying this may not be politically correct, but this lack of respect, this flaunting of authority, is the root of the problem. I recognize that our society teaches and reinforces, even glamorizes, this lack of respect—our movies, our music, our clothing, the drug culture all reinforce the notion that authority is bad and should be resisted at all costs. And here in Boise, Idaho, that lack of respect has now cost us the life of a police officer.

Now, after you have those discussions in your family rooms or around your kitchen tables, I want you to come to a town hall meeting at City Hall on September 30 at 6 p.m. to share your ideas with us.

We want to talk about our community values. We want to talk about our community priorities. We want to talk about our relationship with our police officers. Let us use this opportunity to learn and heal.

I want this community to know that I have complete faith and confidence in Larry Paulson, our chief of police. I want this community to know that I have complete faith and confidence in the City Council's ability to provide oversight and direction to the police. And I want you to know that I have complete faith and confidence that we as a community will find ways to support the family of Mark Stall and to support and respect our police.

Thank you.

Appendix 2

Text of Funeral Speakers

ARNOLD RUBEY

A great sorrow has touched our souls, at times a sorrow far heavier than what the soul seemingly can bear. This sorrow, at least for this family, means the loss of a husband, a father, a son, a brother. For the Boise Police Department, it means the loss of their first in-the-line-of-duty, a team member, an honorable officer, a friend. To this community it means a gifted, respected citizen has laid down his life in the carrying out of his duty.

September twentieth, nineteen hundred and ninety-seven will be a date indelibly etched in our minds and hearts. Mark Arlin Stall, on that date, had a date with destiny whereby he would lay down his life. There comes a recollection of that Friday evening for two little girls with their daddy, before he went off to another night of work. Their together time consisted of them and their daddy dancing to "oldie tunes" and playing freeze. Of a wife having contact with her husband at the midnight hour that night, asking him to forgive her for being grouchy, and of Mark wondering at one point whether this would be another routine night on the beat—*and then the killer's bullet.*

To many of us there is a recollection of Mark Stall as the bigger-than-life kind of guy, always active, always doing, and then the sudden and stark stillness of his absence. As these sorts of things flood our hearts today, I must say in grave seriousness that this overwhelming gathering here this morning is a reminder of our mortality. We live, we die, but we certainly do not expect to die so soon. Parents are not supposed to bury their children, but they do, and with that in your minds I pray that by the time this memorial funeral service ends today, that you will know that the most important thing Mark Stall did in his short life was to prepare for eternity. Therefore the emphasis in this morning hour is not upon his life alone, but upon the God whom he knew and loved.

This occasion is a time for us as a family to thank the caring, compassionate, and grieving Boise Police Department for selfless service to Cheryl and her family in the last five incredibly long days.

Our words are totally inadequate to express how deeply we appreciate all of you and what you have given even further in response to this tragedy. And to this city and community, this family expresses a very grateful heart for your loving compassion. As a community you are here today to pay tribute to an officer and friend, a loving husband, a wonderful father, and that is a remarkable response you have made today. It is now time to stand en masse, shoulder to shoulder, rank after rank, in grateful tribute to the dedicated, brave men and women who are in the trenches for us; and because this is so, I would ask you, out of your sorrow today, to say so.

MAYOR BRENT COLES

This is a difficult experience, to stand in a Pavilion full of sworn police officers, community and state leaders, Governor Batt, legislators, county commissioners, mayors, city council members and other elected officials, knowing that we are being watched live on television by about two million people throughout the northwest; but most importantly here today, we have the family and friends of Mark Stall.

First, let me address our community and Mark's colleagues. Thank you for being here today to honor your friend and one of America's finest examples of a person who believed in his dream and believed he could make a difference, and ultimately accomplished both in his short life. I want to express my appreciation to those who keep us safe, who find our property when it is stolen, who find our kids when they are lost, and who care about our safety and our security.

I asked Cheryl if there was anything she would like me to communicate to the community, and her immediate response was that all Mark wanted in this life was to glorify his Father in heaven. He searched for ways in his life to glorify his Father, and being a police officer was the direction he was given. He was a man of honor and integrity. He loved his family and was committed to their every need. Thank you, Cheryl.

For some reason he was taken, and it is up to us, each individually, to seek to understand. Mark dedicated his life to a greater power, and we can take from his example and also commit our lives, our families, our neighborhoods, our community to a higher cause greater than ourselves—for a purpose more important than our own intellectual prowess, our own physical strength, our own ego, our own political or financial ambition. Ours is a community that gives more than most, so this is a community that hurts more than most when one of our own is taken.

Mark would not want this tragedy to divide our community, but to unite us. So as we search for answers, let us find a way to teach and contemplate the values he stood for. To help us do this as a community, the Boise City Council has committed to naming a future park in Boise after Mark Stall, which will symbolize a place where families and individuals can enjoy our community, but will also be a place of learning and contemplation of Mark's values.

To Cheryl, I have a message from your community. This message was left on a card at the scene of the tragedy by a family I visited there yesterday.

To the Stall family:

> There are no real words to express the loss. We as citizens would like to share our feelings of grief with you. Our community and our young children have lost a very important role model. Our hearts are with you at this time.
> [signed] Jackie and Shirley and families

To Mark's family, you have been blessed to know such a wonderful young person. He must have loved to play cops and robbers—he had such a strong sense of fair play. I am sure he never cheated. In fact, one of his colleagues told Cheryl that when he worked with Mark, everything was by the book.

Cheryl, every spouse of a police officer is praying for you and reaching out to you today. They are looking at their own families and wondering if they could have the strength and courage to endure the loss of their companion. Together we hope that this does not happen again, but even today we know of two more fallen officers in North Carolina.

When I asked our chaplain, Don Peterman, how you were doing, he told me he was with you at the hospital and you had shown great strength and courage. He said you are truly a remarkable person, and he is right. You shared with me that you have felt the Comforter with you and you are being blessed. I want you to know that I believe you have been and will be. I thank you for sharing your strength and courage with me.

When I visited on Saturday night, you and your family lifted my spirit and gave me hope and courage to do what I needed to do in my message to the community on Sunday. As we shared some feelings together, I felt one of the sweetest spirits in your home that I have ever felt in my life. You have in your home a glimpse of what heaven feels like, what it looks like, even what it tastes like.

Now let me share my personal and some very personal thoughts that come from my personal experiences of faith and belief. I want you to know that I believe you will see Mark again and you will be with him. That he misses you and Jonelle and Julia. I know that you had many talks about your dreams and hopes and goals, and your family will find the strength and the path to continue working towards those dreams. Yours is a family that has achieved much over a short period of time, and that same spirit of achievement will give you strength, and you should rely on those talks you had together and the plans you made. In time, that will reduce the sting of Mark's passing. His memory can be a great strength to your family. In Jonelle and Julia you will see Mark every day in their faces. This will be a great source of strength to you and joy to your family. Mark's parents and your parents love you more than words will ever express. Together you feel the grief of his sudden death, together you can share your memories and visions of the future in your children...his children. Your faith and daily prayers will carry you through the challenges that lie ahead in this life and lead you to the next life, where Mark will report to you and you will report to him.

May God bless and keep you safe and keep our community safe likewise, is my prayer.

POLICE CHIEF LARRY PAULSON

Normally you get quite nervous at a time like this...there seems to be somewhat of a calm in my stomach at the moment. I really am honored by the family's request that I speak here today and recognize Mark's service to the community. I would like to say that I appreciate all the support shown here today for the Stall family and the department from all the law enforcement agencies represented here inside this complex, outside, and helping with all the things that go along with this service.

To all the dignitaries, family members, friends, and community supporters that are here today, I thank you. Special appreciation goes out to the Highlanders and to the Boise Police Pipers for their part in this ceremony today, and I would like to recognize that Officer Ron Winegar is here today to join us and at a very difficult time for him. (Applause) Thank you.

Mark's history with law enforcement was a total of eight and one-half years. He spent five years with Los Angeles County, as I understand it, then moved up here because he desired community support and backing by the people that he served. He worked with Ada County for about a half a year, then has been with us, the Boise Police Department, for two, almost three years.

When I was looking at Mark's record, I looked at his birth date, and I was sworn in at Boise Police Department, July 9th—correction, July 8th—1968. It has been too long. Mark was slightly over seven months old at the time. Who would know that we would be here today at the same place, at the same time, for some very tough reasons. I have said before in the department, that I did not want to be the Chief when an officer had fallen in the service of the department, but I find myself here today, and I am really proud to be here.

Mark had a very interesting life, and it was about midway through his life span of twenty-nine years that he kind of developed an interest in law enforcement. He pursued that interest, as you can see by the interest behind him.

He was hired by our department on November 28, 1994, and as I said, brought with him that experience from where he had been elsewhere. He was currently a police officer 2, as far as our grades go, and was working diligently toward advancement in the department. He had a lot of promise to be a future leader in the department as we change in our leadership over the next few years. I have always told everyone when they come into the department, as I was participating in the swearing ceremony, that what an opportunity and what a time to be in service to the City of Boise through the Boise Police Department, because your opportunities were endless in terms of what you wanted to do. He just recently received his advance post certification. I presented that to him in a briefing, and it was just a sign of his continual pursuit of achievement within the department.

I think, personally, Mark was a person who was very meticulous in his personal appearance, the care of his equipment. I think I read somewhere that he would even wipe down his car with his own supplies, both inside and out. He was a very clean person and kept his equipment in top shape.

He had a pleasant personality, and I was talking with some of the dispatchers—from his service with them, they indicated that he was always very willing to step forward and take calls. I don't think they ever heard a grumpy word out of him. That is a lot to be said for an individual who is in a job that isn't always that pleasant. Within his file he had several commendations internally, from the people he worked with, his supervisors, and also citizens.

I find it ironic that Mark was twenty-nine years old, which is approximately the age of the two suspects that he encountered. My question to you is, why did these lives turn out so differently?

Recently, we received some letters from the third grade students at Collister School. I would like to read you just one of those I received. It reads, "Police Department." The spelling is a little different, but very good here. It is the thought that counts. "I'm sorry about Officer Stall's death. I definitely don't like violence. I like them because they help us and sometimes they have to risk their lives." It's signed, "Randy "—I won't give his last name.

You know, I think maybe there's still hope when we have that kind of thought in the young people of our community. I believe that Mark's death should stand for something good. I believe that this is an opportunity for the whole community to get behind a movement to emphasize respect for authority and family values, respect for teachers, respect for law enforcement, and all those that need that. Also, to show an intolerance for lawlessness. I don't believe we have any place for that in the city of Boise.

I am amazed at the strength of Mark's mother and father, but I am most amazed by the strength of Cheryl. It will be needed for your two daughters as they grow up. You must know that Mark will be memorialized forever in the history of the department, and his courage will be an example for others. It will be an encouragement for those who come to the department in the future.

I am proud to have known him, and to Mark I would say, "God bless and farewell."

OFFICER JOHN TERRY

Chief mentioned a couple of points I would just like to go over. He said that Mark kept his car clean. It was always nice to get into Mark's car the next night, after he had the shift before you—spotless!

Before I say a few words about Mark, I would like to say a few words about Cheryl.

I was there that night...I was there...it seemed...and myself and officer Nick Duggan over here, we went to get Cheryl that night. Mark was just still being placed into the paramedic unit that night when we took off to get Cheryl.

We got to the door...to her door...and both of us just stood there shaking.

We both said a little prayer and began knocking on the door. After a short time, Cheryl answered the door...big smile on her face...invited us in. Nick walked in, in front of me. She started asking what was going on. Nick and I just stood there, and Cheryl read our faces. All questions stopped. She just reached out, gave Nick a big hug. She held him for about a minute, and we all cried. She then broke away from Nick and said, "I'll get my clothes. I'll get my clothes on and I'll be ready to go in a minute." Never asking what was going on, she just knew.

This kind of thing is not fun...the kind of thing I've never done before and hope to never do again.

She took care of her children; she got her mother over there to watch them; and we were going out the door before she finally asked what had happened. She turned to me, I told her briefly what I knew, and said, "Mark needs you." She came with us, and we drove her to the hospital that night. She went inside. She went right past the room where they were still working on Mark...sat with the chaplain...waiting.

That's the kind of person she is. She was there for Mark.

I first met Mark when I came to Boise almost three years ago. That first day he took me out to lunch. He and I had both worked in LA and both came to Boise for the same reasons—to find a better way of life and a better place to raise our families.

Mark was truly warm and caring that day, and even helped me fix my truck. I had just had a long trip up here. We immediately became great friends.

Over the next few years, Mark and I worked the graveyard shift together. I saw that Mark was truly a great man. Not because of any flamboyant times he had, but in the measure of his daily work.

He loved God, loved his family, and he loved his job. His priorities were in the right order. He worked hard as a police officer, but that wasn't enough. He had to work a side job on his days off to support his family. When he did take time off, it was to spend quality time with his wife and kids. Now a wife won't have her husband and Mark's children won't have their daddy.

Mark told me how he had a big dance with his six-year-old just hours before he left us. The love in his eyes was evident as his face lit up with pride and joy. He was still celebrating her sixth birthday, and they had danced all around the living room...little angels. He then called home just after midnight to check on his wife and make sure his children were safe in bed.

With so many overgrown boys in this world, Mark was truly a man. A man among men.

Just over an hour later, Mark would be killed, and to his children I would tell you that he will still be watching you. He is no longer a guardian of the streets; he is now your guardian angel.

Several months ago, I, too, was shot by an evil bullet. A few days later, my six-year-old girl came up to me and wanted to tell me a secret. She told me that sometimes bad men shoot you and you don't die. We had a long talk. Then, two days after Mark was killed, she came to me again and told me another secret. She said, "Sometimes bad men shoot you and you do die." Then she begin crying, telling me not to let the bad men kill me. She did not want me to go back to work, fearing I would never come home, "just like Daddy's friend Mark."

I had to hold her awhile and reassure her that I would come home. I then told her that daddy's friend Mark had also gone home. He was with his Heavenly Father and would still be watching after his family forever... forever.

This tragedy affects us all. I'm sure that the same conversation was repeated over and over by all members of law enforcement in this room and by law enforcement everywhere. Not just the night after, but every day before...every day after...it affects us all, like a spider web touches all of us, everyone in this room and all of us in the community. Sons and daughters, wives and husbands, brothers, sisters, grandparents, friends and neighbors, we're all one big community...one big family...it touches everybody.

Mark's death was truly a tragedy—not an accident, not a mistake, but a murder. Not only Mark's death, but a death that touches us all—the murder of a police officer.

Mark died doing what he believed in—what we all believe in. Mark thought he could make a difference, and he did. Like a shining light when the darkest of evil was all around him, Mark stood tall. He stood tall for all that was good. He'd put that uniform on and stood proudly behind that star on his chest—the star that I wear—the star that all police officers wear.

It was a symbol of Mark's dedication and belief that what he was doing was right. Never avoiding danger, but facing danger so that others would not have to, so that people can walk in the streets and so that children could play in the park. Mark was there, wearing that badge, that symbol that he believed in. Evil that night did not know Mark, but saw the uniform and the star, the symbols Mark wore. Evil tried to kill a uniform and a star that night, but got Mark instead. He died proudly, facing danger with his fellow officers; standing for what he believed in and what he loved doing.

I feel that we may look back one day soon, in the future, and see this as a pivotal point in time, where good and decent people took the time to stand up and be counted. I know Mark did.

I would like to share with you some of the events that early Saturday morning. I was there. The smoke was still heavy in the air, and the sounds of the battlefield, and it was a battlefield, echoed all around. As I approached, I ran through that battlefield, searching for the evil that was there. The evil had passed, but had left its mark. Seven men stood before evil, but now there were only six.

I ran to see if I could help. "Two officers down," was the radio call I had just heard seconds earlier around the corner—seconds away, but not close enough. Ron Winegar was hit and being helped by another officer. I quickly ran to see who else had been hit. I knew everyone there.

I saw Rob Berrier, Mark's partner that night, holding Mark in his arms, crying. It was already too late. Mark was leaving us. As my little girl said, "His spirit was flying up to heaven."

Mark did not avoid danger that night, but faced danger. He continued facing that danger, that extreme violence. I talked to the men there, to listen to their story; to listen to find out how and why Mark had died.

As he fell under a hail of gunfire, his own partner, Rob Berrier, began dragging Mark out from the line of fire. Even as the bullets continued whizzing by both men, he continued to drag Mark out of the line of fire. Mark was already fatally wounded, shot through the heart, and didn't even know it. He didn't cry out; he didn't scream in pain...he continued doing... continued doing what he chose to do, wearing that symbol, that star, that uniform.

What Mark didn't know was that he and his partner were still facing danger. Mark continued shooting, still trying to protect himself and his partners from the awful violence.

Rob Berrier was trying to give him first aid. Mark lay there watching; watching for the evil. Keep it away from his partner, while his partner tended to him. He gave his life for his partners that night, fighting for what he believed in.

A few weeks ago I received a Medal of Valor for bravery. I would just like to say to Cheryl and Mark that Mark can't wait for a ceremony, so I'm going to give him my medal. He deserves it.

To Mark Stall, for his courage and his willingness to enforce the law in the face of grave personal danger, I award you my Medal of Honor. (*Note: As the audience stood in applause, John Terry walked from the platform to Mark's casket and placed his medal on a portrait of Mark Stall resting on the casket. He then turned and embraced Cheryl Stall.*)

DETECTIVE ALAN HARDWICK

We've come here today to honor the life of a wonderful man. Mark Stall was a man who was full of life. He lived more in twenty-nine years than most of us even dream of. He was vivacious, energetic, highly skilled, professional, courageous. He had many good qualities, many of which you've heard already. He was one of the best fathers I have ever known.

Mark's days weren't always easy, although you wouldn't know it. He had a very good attitude about the hard days. I know that sometimes when he would work a day shift and come home...I had the opportunity to come home with him a couple of times after a difficult day...and he'd see his little Julia. He'd say, " Ju! Ju! Ju! Ju!"

He didn't bring his work home.

Mark was a very strong, loving, understanding husband. He cared for his wife...consistently.

He was a very friendly man.

He was a very funny man.

We all enjoyed him.

Somebody recently said that he was the kind of friend that you want to have. He certainly was. He'd give you anything. He'd do anything for anyone. And I've heard stories this week from the family that broadened my understanding of that.

Mark worked hard at being the best that he could be in everything he did. Nothing was done halfway. If it was worth doing, it was worth doing it right, doing it well.

He was a man dedicated to service and excellence.

Scripture says, "...whatever you do, do them as unto the Lord." And that is what Mark Stall did.

Mark Stall did not do things in excellence so that he would be lifted up high and praised. That wasn't his focus. That wasn't even a side thought.

It's true that he is honored, and he was honored and he was respected, as he is now. But the reasons that brought him that respect were not founded in a hope that he would be publicly honored and put forth, as "this is the one, this is the kind of man we need to look to and follow." Mark did all that he did to the glory of God, not to the praise of Mark.

As I have visited with Cheryl over the last few days, it has been her expressed wish that all that goes on here today and that will take place later today, would be to the glory and praise of God, and God alone.

That was his desire, to see God praised.

Mark believed the words of the Lord Jesus that said, "...anyone who wishes to be great, must first be the servant of all." The profession that we are in, many of us here—peace officer, public servant—for many that's just a series of words, but not for Mark. He was a true servant. He was a servant of his God. Mark served God in the way that he raised his children. He served God in the way he loved his wife. He served God in the way he honored his father and mother, and the way that he loved his neighbors and the way that he encouraged his friends. Everything that he did was in service of God.

And many of us do not remember Mark Stall as a man who "crammed the Bible down your throat," as they say; and he didn't. He lived the Scriptures. They were his worldview. They were a part of his life, his core being. God had made Mark Stall what he is, and Mark served Him well. You have all seen Mark's faith put into practice, perhaps without knowing it. Now at the end of his life, Mark is with the One who created him.

Like in the Bible, in the 25th chapter of Matthew, God tells His servants, "Enter the kingdom...prepared for you from the foundation of the world... For I was hungry and you gave me food. I was thirsty and you gave me something to drink. I was naked and you clothed me. I was a stranger and you took me in. I was sick and you visited me. I was in prison and you came to me."

And in answer to that, I'm sure that Mark, as a righteous man would say, "When did I do these things? I didn't do enough—I needed to do more. I wanted to do more." Mark always wanted to help.

And the night that Mark Stall died, he was doing that very thing.

He wasn't the first car there—he was in the back of the herd. He was one of the last people there, and then he ran to the front and took the fire from other officers. And that would be far better than good enough, but no! He wasn't done. Like John said, even after fatally wounded, he reached around Rob's back and continued to fire back...because he was trying to help.

Mark Stall was a servant.

He was a servant.

He was a great father.

He was my first true friend here in Boise, and he did all these things because he loved the Lord, his God, and so now he is honored.

BROTHERS AND SISTERS:
LOUISE

Well, my stomach doesn't feel quite as good as the Chief's does, so I hope you'll bear with me.

There is one person that we know who would have loved a celebration like this and can't be here, and that's our brother, Mark. As we brothers and sisters sat around last night thinking of what we wanted to say to all of you, we laughed and laughed while remembering Mark.

We couldn't help but remember the fun times we had as a family, like our houseboat trips to Lake Shasta, where Mark barefooted off the top of the houseboat. The long hours he spent teaching our children how to water-ski. Even when their parents and Grandpa had run out of patience, Mark hung in there until the task had been mastered.

And that guy loved Christmas. He would play Christmas music in July, and he had to have the brightest tree in town—some six hundred and fifty lights, I think, was his record.

If anyone could tell a story, it was Mark. He could capture you with his very first word and keep you enthralled to the very end. You may have forgotten the beginning of the story by then, but I guarantee he kept you entertained the entire way through.

As the sister closest to Mark in age, we spent much time together growing up. We spent countless hours in the back yard making mud pies, jumping curbs on our bikes, riding our bikes to the mall, and late nights talking.

As I have processed this tragedy over the last couple of days, I've been reminded of the importance of family, of making sure that we make things a priority in our life that are closest to our hearts. So often we get wrapped up in the business of our lives that we neglect the ones that really matter.

I'm gonna miss Mark's voice on the phone, saying, "Hey, Sis, whatcha doin'?"

I never realized how hard it would be to put my thoughts and feelings into words. I certainly know Mark wouldn't have had a problem doing that, though. I guess my heart is, that the heartache that we all feel is going to be difficult for many months to come. But the Lord has told me over and over again, Louise, it is not for you to understand, but for you to trust Me. And that is what I've chosen to do.

God has given me a verse last week that spoke dearly to me then, and now has given me even more comfort.

"Peace I leave with you, My peace I give to you. Not as the world gives, but as I give. Do not let your heart be troubled, and do not be afraid."

MATT

As I struggle to make sense of the loss of my brother these last few days, wondering why his life was taken at such a young age, all that makes sense to me is Mark's job here was done before ours.

Since I've been in Boise, I've learned the impact his life has had on other officers, friends, and people he hadn't met yet. For that I am proud.

Mark, you will be deeply missed.

We have lost a great friend.

LINDA

As Mark's oldest sister, I wasn't around him as much as some of the others; but as we spent our time last night, laughing and enjoying being together, the void of him not being with us was strongly felt. Mark loved to have fun.

Whenever there was a family "get-together," like a birthday party or an anniversary for Mom and Dad or birthday party for a niece or nephew, Mark did everything he could to be there, sometimes surprising us at the last moment. Mark loved his family.

We had the real wonderful luxury in our home to be raised close. We spent family vacations every year doing all kinds of interesting things, going to very many different places, and we grew together.

I know Mark, and that was his goal for his family—to spend time teaching his girls, and whoever else maybe would have come along, the enjoyment that sisters and brothers and parents can have.

We learned to enjoy each other even to this day, just like spending the wee hours of this morning being together and laughing even in spite of our sadness.

We know that Mark would have loved to be with us, and I would just encourage you as I know, if Mark was standing here, to just take a second look at your family and look at some special value in them. Take your kids on a special trip or just dance around the living room with them this afternoon, and give them a special hug. I'd really like to thank you, from all of us, the sisters and brothers, for being special to Mark, as he was special to us, and we're really glad you're here to celebrate his life with us today.

LOUISE

I just thought of saying this, and I just wanted to say, Cheryl, you are always gonna be a part of us and we love you lots.

FATHER:
RAY STALL

Oh, what a task I have to take care of for a minute there, but bear with me, if you will please. I just want to say a little family thing here. Last night... was too...they were out sitting...trying...re-...and going over their thoughts. They were kind of laughing and...just like old times. Just one little thing different...one member of the family was missing. Mom came tromping up the stairs and said, "You kids be quiet! It's late and people are trying to sleep!" (Laughter)

But I would like to first of all, on behalf of my family, thank the City of Boise and the people of Boise for the tribute they are showing my son. And the loving concerns that you have expressed to my family. Especially would like to take time to thank the Boise Police Department and their wives for all they have done in this difficult time for both of us. Captain [meaning Chief Paulson], you have a fantastic group of men and women.

Now, I'd like to take just a few minutes and talk about my son. When my kids were growing up and going to school, I always told them that high grades were not the most important thing. Today, you know, kids always critique the way they were raised, their parents, and I'm told now that maybe sometimes I was not strong enough. Maybe I didn't push them hard enough in the academic areas, but something that I did tell them, that they better not come home with bad reports in deportment or anything that would be dishonest. Today I believe it has paid off, from what I have heard in the last few days, since I've been in Boise.

Those of you that know Mark—maybe those of you who were stopped by him during his work—know he could and would talk. Well, I have a little thing to tell you. He hardly spoke a word in public until he was five years old! In fact, the pastor of our church at that time would say, "You know that kid won't talk to anybody but his mother, not even his father!" That was really true, especially in public.

You know his brothers and sisters would often joke with him by saying, "Boy, we really don't want to get pulled over by you. We really don't want to listen to your lecture. Mark, just give us a ticket without all the talk!" But you know, these last few days, as people come up to me when I've been on the streets, down at the scene, the mortuary, wherever, I see those lectures really did affect a lot of peoples lives.

I want to tell you about a couple of incidents, if I could for just a moment. I'll try to do them briefly.

On Sunday, we had a request to do a brief television interview. The reporter introduced himself and turned to introduce us to the cameraman. The cameraman said to me, "You know, I knew your son. He was a good friend of mine. I really enjoyed him. We had good times having coffee together."

I said, "Great, how did you meet my son?"

He said, "He gave me a ticket!"

That's quite a compliment, I think, from a man given a ticket and still befriended by another man.

I had the privilege of riding with Mark on several occasions, every time I'd get an opportunity, when he was in Los Angeles and since he's come to Boise. I'd always try to get a "ride-along" with him. We were here in May and had a ride-along with him. It happened to be on graduation night, and about two or three o'clock in the morning got a call that there had been a slight automobile accident up on Hill road. We went...a couple of other officers were there first...taking care of all the business that needed to be done, and they said, "Mark, would you wrap it up?"

Mark took this teenage girl off to the side and started asking her some questions. Asked her where she had been; she was really the one at fault in the accident. She said that she had been at a party just down the street, down the side street from where the accident happened. He asked was there any liquor at that party, and she said yes. And he said did you have anything to drink and she kind of...kind of evasively waltzed and danced around that. And in Mark's unique way, he said, "How many drinks did you have? One? Two? Three? Four? It's really not a very hard question to answer." She came back; I really don't remember the number. He began to ask her if she really knew what the legal blood alcohol content...alcohol percentage was. She told him a number. He said no, that wasn't correct, and he went on to tell her what the number was and that she was a teenager, and all of the things, the problems that she could create. He gave her a sobriety test, and said you know, you really shouldn't have been driving. This took only a few minutes, I don't remember how long. He reached over and began to write, and she said, "You're not going to give me a ticket, also!"

He said, "Yes, I am. Because the next time you go to a party, maybe it will help you to think about what the consequences might be. Maybe you'll make the right decision."

You know Mark, as it's already been mentioned, did have a sense of humor. It started very young in life. I remember an incident when he was either six or seven, at home. His sister, Linda, whom you just heard, was sick one evening. She was in the bathroom on her knees in front of the toilet, throwing up, and at that time she had long hair, so she was holding her hair back from falling in her face with her hands. Mark came to the door and stuck his head in the door and said, "Hey, Linda, are you afraid it's gonna come out of your ears?"

That's...that's my son.

Mark was particular; it's already been mentioned also. In fact some...in fact most of us would say that he was a perfectionist. When he was about twelve, thirteen, or fourteen years old, he said, "Mom, you really don't put my stuff away in the drawer the way I'd like it. You know I like things nice and neat. Uh, Mom—just set the stuff on the bed from now on, and I'll put it away myself."

That was my Mark, right, Cheryl?

You know he became interested in law enforcement because of an event in his life when he was sixteen years old. I'm not going to go into the details of that; there was a bit in a piece in the paper yesterday. But that event made Mark at that time decide to prepare himself to be a law enforcement officer. He started studying even in high school psychology and began working, taking classes over at the junior college very close to our home...he went away...went away to college to prepare himself for the profession that he really wanted.

You know he loved his job. He loved helping people—helping them on the job, away from the job. You know he was very, very proud of his job. And he took it extremely seriously.

I'd just like to say one more thing. It's been also mentioned before but, as a father, I'd like to tell you, Mark loved the Lord. He knew Jesus as his own personal Savior. He had a strong relationship with his Savior, and there was no doubt in his mind what eternity meant to him. And I just want to... just as our Heavenly Father gave His Son for all of us, I trust that my son may help in just reaching...just a few more.

Mark, you're a great son and we're very proud of you. You know, sometimes we don't say that enough as parents. We were very proud of you. You gave us great joy and you'll be greatly missed. 1042 (ending tour of duty).

PASTOR DAVID MADDOX

In just a moment I'm going to read Scripture and have a word of prayer, but before I do that let me just mention that I believe it is fitting that we read from the Bible. The Word of God was a lamp unto Mark's feet and a light to his path. Mark knew the Scripture, as you have heard many times already, as a very faithful and trusting guide to his life. I preached from this Scripture some eight years ago, September 2nd, at Mark and Cheryl's wedding, charging them at that time to live for the LORD and to serve Him, a charge which they have been faithful to this entire time. Also, it is fitting that I read from this particular copy of the Scripture—this is Mark's personal Bible. And if you were to see it, you would see that it is worn and filled with notes and highlight marks, as Mark spent time studying the Scripture.

He loved the Word of God, but more importantly, he loved and knew the Author of this book. And finally, I think that it is fitting that I read from the Psalms. Though separated by many centuries, I think that Mark and King David of Israel had much in common. Like King David, Mark was commissioned with the awesome responsibility to protect and to serve. Mark stood against those that were unruly and lawless. Both King David of Israel and Mark were willing and capable officers of the law. Both men served noble things, as you have heard—things like truth, and that which is right, and justice, and righteousness.

Mark commanded admiration and respect from all who knew him, and you have heard that this afternoon: for his love and his care which he exhibited to his wife and to his children; for his patriotism; for his sound judgment, his personal courage, and his gentle humor; his spotless integrity; his keen sense of honor and his willingness to sacrifice for others; and for his patient submission to the providences of God.

Listen to these words from King David, the sweet Psalmist of Israel. I've selected some verses out of the many verses that Mark has highlighted in his Bible. Listen to them, because I think they echo Mark's heart.

Do not fret because of evildoers, for they will wither quickly like the grass. But trust in the Lord and do good and then you will dwell in the land and cultivate faithfulness. Delight yourself in the Lord and He will give you the desires of your heart. Commit your way to the Lord, trust also in Him and He will bring forth your righteousness as the light and your judgment as the noon day.

And another verse he had highlighted says, " Rest in the Lord and wait patiently for Him."

In another place, "The steps of a good man are established by the Lord and God delights in his way." And, "When a good man falls he will not be hurled headlong, because the Lord is the one who holds his hand."

How blessed are those who dwell in Thy house, O God. How blessed is the man whose strength is the Lord, for a day in Your court is better than a thousand outside. I would rather stand at the threshold of the house of God, than dwell in the tents of the wicked. For the Lord God is a sun and a shield. The Lord gives grace and glory and no good thing does He withhold from those who walk uprightly. How blessed is the man who trusts in Thee, O God.

And then, let me just read one passage that Mark has highlighted in the New Testament—a passage that is familiar in times like this; a passage that is intended to comfort and console and to give hope; a passage that is a quote from our Lord Jesus Christ in John 14.

Let not your heart be troubled, believe in God and believe also in Me. In My Father's house are many dwelling places, and if it were not so I would have told you. For I go to prepare a place for you. And if I go, and prepare a place for you I will come again and receive you unto Myself. That where I am, there you may also be.

Let's pray together.

Father, we pause and by our very posture, with our heads bowed and our eyes closed, we honor You and give thanks to You for your servant, your child, Mark Arlin Stall. Mark was and forever will be Your child. He was, above all else, your servant. He was a loving son and devoted husband, a faithful father, a courageous officer, a decisive leader; and, Lord, we have heard this afternoon that in all things, he was a stirring example to those around him. We thank You for that, because it is evidence of Your presence in his life and the work You performed in him.

In all his endeavors, Mark's life spoke of a deep love for his Heavenly Father and Lord. We know and have confidence that comes to us from this very book which I have read from, that right now, Mark is where You are. But in a very real way he is not gone from us, because he still lives in his wife and Jonelle and Julia, and both in life and death, Mark changed us. What You made him to be and what he stood for left their imprint on us. His life left Your imprint on us. Thank you, Lord. Mark was a special gift from You. He served You well. In Christ's name we pray. Amen.

ARNOLD RUBEY

Mark, my son, you were too young to die.

Cheryl, my girl, you are too young to be a widow.

Jonelle and Julia, my precious granddaughters, you are too young to be without your daddy; but God in the mystery of His unfathomable providence, allowed all of this to be.

In my humanness, I want to cry out and say this was unnecessary. Someone so valuable to so many has been removed so needlessly by a sudden and deadly violence, quickly snuffed out by an unnecessary bullet, so it seems to me and many of you like me.

Yet it is all reality without the possibility of change. We cannot go back and undo. My son-in-law will not, cannot come home here again.

Somehow, someway, it seems that God lost this one. He surely could have made a deadly bullet, undeadly; preserved one of His own and saved him for his family and his community. But He didn't, and so the mystery arises as to why. I want to be so bold today as to suggest to you a possibility as to why. To do so, I first read to you the words of Isaiah 55, which say from God: "'My thoughts are not your thoughts, Nor are your ways My ways,' says the LORD. 'For as the heavens are higher than the earth, So are My ways higher than your ways, and My thoughts from your thoughts.'"

There is a grand design in the mystery of God's providence, a design so unique that only He could shape it to accomplish divine purposes. Often, then, of course, those designs go contrary to what we desire or want. Often they leave us bewildered. We yearn to know why the Almighty allows painful or wicked happenings to touch us, or certain people to take from us that which we cherish.

In this case God allowed two young men, virtually the same age as our Mark, to perpetrate acts which cost Mark's life and their own. I cannot speak for them and their lives, or even their destiny, but I can for Mark's. Mark was prepared, as you've heard; He was prepared for eternity because he had embraced the wonders of God's saving grace in his own life. This centers upon why Mark may have been selected to pay such a price, to fulfill a certain design of God.

Now, I'm rather certain that you might reason that this is a cruel suggestion, that God would surely not do such a thing. For what reason would God do this or allow this? Just this—the most important aspect of man does not rest in the temporal elements of his mortality, but with the eternal elements, with the things that matter most; and I boldly declare to you today, that what matters most to me as a grieving parent is that I know where Mark is.

He is at home in heaven, where he made prior preparations; and because he was prepared, it would be better to be an officer, a man, a soul, ready to meet God.

I look upon you this day, the many law enforcement people in this great building. It moves me beyond description to see all of you gathered in this setting and in this way. We all honor and salute you, and rightly; but I now want to ask you a question of greater importance than what your uniform represents—your code, your commitment to justice. Were it you, rather than Mark, would you have been ready? Do you know now that you are ready? I likewise look upon the balance of this vast audience, and I ask, are you ready for eternity?

The importance of eternal matters exceeds the value of your business or your earthly commitments. It is greater than your possessions or your treasures here. It is the biggest issue of all.

Solomon, the gifted and wise son of David who has been referred to in the Old Testament, spoke to the necessity of understanding eternity. In Ecclesiastes 3, he made two sobering statements.

1. Speaking of God—He has put eternity in their hearts.
2. Whatever God does, shall be forever.

Because God is a forever kind of God, you need to be a forever kind of person, one who responds to His presence and to His mercy. And I can say that to you today because I know, because we were so close. We lived in the same home for an extended period of time, my wife and I, Mark and Cheryl, and two precious granddaughters, side by side in the same environment. I know...I know what made Mark the man he was, and it was more than a striving to be ethical and honest and hard working. It was God.

He saw beyond now to see then, and I want to tell you that never does that preparation mean more to this family than in this present hour of sorrow. This family grieves, but not as those who lack hope. They shed their tears from broken hearts, because of the pain; but they know this cherished son, husband, dad, brother, and cousin, is where there is no more death, no more sorrow, no more crying, no more pain. He is, as the old hymn writer wrote, "Safe in the arms of

Jesus, Safe on His gentle breast, There by His love o'er shaded, Sweetly, my soul shall rest."

I leave one other statement, from Isaiah 55: "So shall My word be that goes forth from My mouth. It shall not return to me void, but it shall prosper in the thing for which I sent it."

We're back to the mystery of God's providence, that He can take the tragedies of life, the sorrows that pain us to where we sometimes think we cannot face another day; in which our aching hearts say, "Why?" But God, through a sorrowful pathway of suffering here, is sending forth a message. I believe on this very day, in this very place, in this very setting, in these tragic circumstances, God is sending a message that says, "Prepare to meet me."

He is using His word to speak to all of us. May we be ready listeners; oh yea, more than that, ready hearers. And therein lies the key to God's mysterious providence; and while we cannot see through the tears, or understand through the darkened veil, these things, God nevertheless is causing to prosper that which fulfills His purposes.

He's different from us, and wiser. He is stronger and more tempered. He is exceedingly merciful and forgiving, and I cherish that kind of savior, because He is just what I need in my brokenness. And we must be willing, as was Mark, to trust Him with our souls. And so God lifted from this life a young man in the prime of life with a loving family, in the mystery of His great providence. He took home a son, a husband, a daddy; but I want to say to you today, friends, join with this family and join with Mark in anchoring your soul in the eternal haven of rest.

We miss Mark, but we still have His God, and because of that we can have hope that goes beyond the veil of death.

Is it well with your soul?

Appendix 3

BRODRICK BROTHERS STOLE SOMETHING IRREPLACEABLE ON SEPT. 20

Idaho Statesman newspaper editorial, December 14, 1997

The shot that killed officer Mark Stall wreaked havoc upon many lives.

Since September 20, I have been daily forced to cope with the ramifications of the death of my son-in-law, Mark Stall. Likewise every other member of this family deals with this tragedy, each in his or her own way.

I can say that I have found a strong measure of comfort in my conviction that God, in His divine and unfathomable wisdom, has not erred nor allowed this sorrow without a specific purpose. In fact, countless lives have been deeply impacted, redirected and changed in numerous ways. This has been confirmed by the receipt of literally hundreds of cards, letters, calls and comments from across the country. This is heartening, even in the time of sorrow.

In another sense, I also cope with the not-so-heartening conclusion that this loss of Mark's life was utterly unnecessary. Everybody lost something irreplaceable that morning.

Two brothers, also left dead and undoubtedly thrusting their own family into anguish, initiated actions that became injurious and fatal. A person may do his own thing, make foolish choices if he wants, even foolishly waste himself if he chooses, but it is far more consequential when drawing others into potential or actual harm. In this case, these men wreaked havoc upon many lives, including their own, because of their destructive mind-set.

219

Their choices that morning cost everyone on the scene and many others not on the scene. They stole away a man's life who did not deserve to die and left an indelible image etched in other officers' minds of their own team member and friend needlessly dying before them.

John Terry accurately stated at Mark's funeral, "Evil tried to kill a uniform and star that night, but it got Mark instead." As a result, neither this police department nor this family can ever restore what was taken from them that awful morning hour. In retrospect, this is what the Brodrick brothers did in the darkness of September 20:

They senselessly and violently destroyed a man's life by killing him.

They stole a husband from his wife.

They took a loving daddy from his two young daughters.

They stripped a cherished son from his parents.

They removed a respected and loved man from the rest of his family.

They callously destroyed one who was a special friend to many people.

They deposed an honorable police officer from the city of Boise.

They usurped a sense of well being from this community by their senseless act.

They put several other officers in harm's way, forcing them to defend their lives.

They breached another officer's physical well being by also shooting him.

They unwittingly but decidedly placed the Boise Police Department on trial once again in the arena of public opinion—to be second-guessed and verbally pillaged by ready-and-waiting gainsayers who amazingly create excuses for, and even justify the defiance of, people like the Brodricks. The violent acts of these brothers notwithstanding, the critics then have no one left to blame but the police. I must admit my bewilderment at such reasoning.

In their short stay in Boise, these two young men gave nothing to the community, but ended up taking much from it. They ravaged a family who now bear the irreversible consequences of their violence for the rest of their lives and left the community wondering why.

Let us not lose sight of who set up and initiated this scenario. Alert and savvy officers, making a legitimate traffic stop, shortly thereafter sensed something further unfolding, and rightfully requested backup. In a matter of moments, they are forced to take deadly action. The result to them? The pain of living with the results of this tragedy for the rest of their lives.

Those who glibly think Boise policemen are trigger-happy cowboys ought to consider what these officers emotionally deal with after they did what they had to do that night. In this case, they suffer even more because of the loss of a friend and fellow officer. They have no notches on their guns, but they do have scars in their hearts, which will never be wiped away.

Let us remember that these officers were doing precisely what we expect of them each time they go to work in our community—help protect us. When they enter harm's way as they did September 20, they hold the responsibility and right to protect the community at large—and yes, they have the right to defend their own lives. The extensive weaponry and other potentially destructive items found in the living quarters of the Brodricks afterward tell me our officers may have prevented an even more disastrous incident later on.

Therefore, these honorable officers have nothing to hide or hang their heads over—they did what we expect of them if evil confronts them. Those who readily and easily criticize their actions ought to try placing themselves in their shoes and role play if necessary, what they would do, were they confronted with what these officers faced. I suspect their response would be very similar to what in fact happened that morning if they wished to stay alive.

In the end, the Brodrick brothers were thieves—they stole the most precious thing they could—life from one who deserved to live. They further stole from family and friends and from all who were unknowingly protected night after night by Mark Stall. They also paid with their lives—what a waste.

Arnold Rubey of Boise is the father-in-law of Boise Police Officer Mark Stall.

Appendix 4

Delivered by Gregory S. Casey, Sergeant-at-arms, U.S. Senate to the tenth Annual Awards Ceremony of the United States Capitol Police, Friday, December 5, 1997

In the early morning hours of September 20, 1997, police officer Mark Stall was shot and killed by a random bullet in a gunfight with a couple of thugs.

He lost his life on a street in the town where I was born and raised; where my father was born and raised; where my grandfather was born and raised.

On a street where I used to deliver newspapers.

He was a member of the same police department that sponsored the explorer scout post where I earned some of scouting's highest honors.

He was a law enforcement colleague of my father and brother-in-law.

I did not know officer Stall—never met him.

But officer Stall was the first law enforcement officer to die in the line of duty in the history of the police department of my hometown of Boise, Idaho.

While this story is repeated over and over and over every year in this nation, it is never an easy story to tell.

And you may wonder what this has to do with you today.

Indeed, it has everything to do with—us! You and me and what we do.

I did not come to this position as a law enforcement professional, as the House Sergeant at Arms and his deputy did.

Prior to this job, I did not have the opportunity to work with you.

Like most Americans, I looked upon those who wear the uniform of law enforcement with awe and respect, rarely understanding what it was that peace officers actually do to keep that peace.

But my exposure to the Boise City Police as a youngster led to the conclusion that peace officers are the backbone of my community.

Without their efforts, the community I knew and loved would not have been the same.

In a very real sense, the men and women of the Capitol Hill Police are the community police of our nation.

They have served this building and grounds for well over a hundred years, and in recent years they have transformed into one of the nation's finest.

Our K-nine unit is unsurpassed.

Our anti-snipers are both the best and second best in the nation.

We win at patrol officer competitions.

And we win at many, many other law enforcement competitions.

But winning awards is less important than winning the trust, the respect, and the hearts and minds of the American people.

When they held the funeral for Officer Stall in Boise, Idaho, on September 24th of this year, some three thousand people attended [actual attendance was at least double that figure].

Most of them didn't know Officer Stall.

They knew the uniform, and what it meant to their way of life.

That's why the story of Officer Mark Stall is important to all of you.

You now set the standard of law enforcement as America's community police.

For millions of Americans who come here every year, you symbolize law and order in America.

You also protect an entire branch of government, without which our republic would not exist.

This is the legacy you have inherited.

But just as your own success follows on the record and in the footsteps of those who went before, you are leaving an even more profound legacy of your own.

I congratulate each and every one of you for the jobs well done.

Of the countless duties that go with my position, I am the most proud of being the Chairman of the U.S. Capitol Police.

That is the legacy you have given me.

That is the legacy law enforcement officers leave the public all across America every day.

You should be most proud of that legacy—of that service.

I salute you—

On behalf of the Board of the U.S. Capitol Police

On behalf of the members and leaders of the U.S. Senate

On behalf of that little boy who grew up to admire those men and women in blue who created community he loved

On behalf of the American people

And in the memory of Officer Mark Stall and hundreds of others who similarly gave their ultimate for the safety of others.

Best wishes—God bless you, and thank you for what you do.

(Note: Less than eight months after this speech, the first line-of-duty deaths in the U.S. Capitol Police occurred. Two officers were killed inside the U.S. Capitol.)

Appendix 5

Congressional Record

THURSDAY, MAY 14, 1998
SENATE
NATIONAL PEACE OFFICERS MEMORIAL DAY
MAY 14, 1998

Mr. Kempthorne - Mr. President, I stand today as the sponsor of Senate Resolution 201 designating May 15, 1998, as National Peace Officers Memorial Day.

This is the fifth year in a row that I have sponsored this resolution, and I am proud to be joined this year by sixty-two of my Senate colleagues in honoring the brave men and women who serve this country as peace officers.

These individuals who serve this nation as our guardians of peace do so at great personal risk. There are few communities in America that have not been touched by the senseless death of a peace officer by violent means. Last year, two communities in Idaho experienced the tragic deaths of two very talented and brave officers. I would like to share with you the sacrifices these men gave to protect the sanctity of their communities. It is my hope that while I relay their stories, each of us would realize the important role that peace officers play in our everyday lives.

While searching for the body of an 18-month old infant who had been lost in the Salmon River, William Inman, a Lemhi County Sheriff, was killed when his hyper-light aircraft struck an unmarked power line and he tragically plunged into the river.

Deputy Inman devoted his entire life to being an excellent police officer. He was a Sergeant in the police force in Peoria, Illinois, where he retired in order to become Chief of Police in Farmington, Illinois. After retiring from the Farmington force he moved to Salmon, Idaho, where he went to work as Sheriff's Deputy for Lemhi County. After his death Chief Inman was inducted posthumously into the American Police Hall of Fame.

William Inman was a father of four children: Maria, Tracy, Jeff, and Jennifer, and was a loving husband to his wife Donna. Along with spending as much time with his family as he could, William was an avid outdoorsman.

The second tragedy struck Idaho's State Capitol of Boise in the early morning hours of September 20, 1997. Boise Police Officer Mark Stall pulled over a car bearing Pennsylvania plates that had committed a traffic violation. The driver and passenger of the vehicle were refusing to cooperate with Officer Stall's requests, when the driver suddenly removed a gun from under his coat and shot Officer Stall. Stall, inflicted with a mortal gunshot wound, fell back to his patrol vehicle for cover and continued firing at the men in order to protect other Boise Officers in the ensuing gunfight. Both Officer Mark Stall and the two assailants were killed. Stall's sacrifice, however, protected not only the officers at the scene but the community as well, when a search of the suspects' residence revealed an arsenal of guns and explosive materials.

Officer Stall was an exemplary police officer and set the standard for other officers both in Boise and around the nation. He was a loving father to his daughters Jonelle and Julia, and a devoted husband and best friend to his wife Cheryl. Officer Stall was committed to his family, his community, his job, and above all his God. I would like to share with you an excerpt from the Idaho Statesman article that outlines the lives of Idaho Peace Officers. In the article Officer Heath Compton characterized his hero, Mark Stall. "One night quite a while back, I was driving down State Street in my patrol car, when a Boise police officer shined his spotlight in my face. I stopped to talk with him. I had never met the officer before, but realized quickly that he was very likable. He introduced himself as Mark Stall. Over the next several months, I got to know Mark quite well. What I learned was that Mark loved God, his family, and the people he worked for and with. He always had a smile on his face and a good word."

The bravery and commitment to community that these men possessed will be carried on by their families. I am pleased to say that I have had the opportunity to spend time with the families of both officers, and I am proud that some of them could join me in the Senate gallery today. The strength and perseverance that is exemplified by each of them is an inspiration to me. My thoughts and prayers go out to these families and others that have been devastated by this type of senseless loss.

This resolution is not the answer to the meaningless violence that occurs in our communities, but it is a small attempt to celebrate and memorialize the lives of the officers. I would like to thank my colleagues for their co-sponsorship and would like to again thank the officers and the families that have come from all fifty states to our nation's Capitol on this special day to eulogize these officers that have given the greatest sacrifice of all, their lives, in the performance of their duties.

(Note: Senator Kempthorne's available information on some of the details of this incident is at variance with the actual happening itself. However, the overall scenario is what matters.)

Safely Home

I am home in Heaven, dear ones;
Oh, so happy and so bright!
There is perfect joy and beauty
In this everlasting light.
All the pain and grief is over,
Every restless tossing passed;
I am now at peace forever,
Safely home in Heaven at last.
Did you wonder I so calmly
Trod the valley of the shade?
Oh! But Jesus' love illumined
Every dark and fearful glade.
And He came Himself to meet me
In that way so hard to tread;
And with Jesus' arm to lean on,
Could I have one doubt or dread?
Then you must not grieve so sorely,
For I love you dearly still:
Try to look beyond earth's shadows,
Pray to trust our Father's will.
There is work still waiting for you,
So you must not idly stand;
Do it now, while life remaineth—
You shall rest in Jesus' land.
When that work is all completed,
He will gently call you Home;
Oh, the rapture of that meeting,
Oh, the joy to see you come!

This poem quoted from *Knight's Treasury of Illustrations* (Eerdmans Publishing Company, Grand Rapids, MI, 1963). No author listed.

Order Form

Postal orders:
Arnold Rubey, P.O. Box 97 Eagle, ID 83616

Telephone orders: (888) 588-8915

Please send *Fallen Brother in Blue* **to:**

Name:_____

Address:_____

City:_____ State:_____

Zip:_____

Telephone: (_____) _____

Book Price: $15.00 in U.S. dollars.

Sales Tax: Please add 5.0% for books shipped to an Idaho address.

Shipping: $3.00 for the first book and $1.00 for each additional book to cover shipping and handling within US, Canada, and Mexico. International orders add $6.00 for the first book and $2.00 for each additional book.

Quantity Discounts Available - Please call for information